THE POWER OF DUFF

Stephen Belber

BROADWAY PLAY PUBLISHING INC
New York
www.broadwayplaypub.com
info@broadwayplaypub.com

Cover photo by Michael Lamont

First edition: May 2022
I S B N: 978-0-88145-922-7

Book design: Marie Donovan
Page make-up: Adobe InDesign
Typeface: Palatino

THE POWER OF DUFF was first produced at the Geffen Playhouse in Los Angeles, running from 7 April-17 May 2015. The cast and creative contributors were:

CHARLES DUFF (CHARLIE) .... Josh Stamberg
SUE RASPELL .... Elizabeth Rodriguez
                                                 Yetta Gottesman
JOHN EBBS .... Brendan Griffin
SCOTT ZOELLNER .... Eric Ladin
RICK .... Tanner Buchanan
CASEY .... Maurice Williams
RON KIRKPATRICK & others .... Joe Paulik

Director .... Peter DuBois
Scenic Designer .... Clint Ramos
Costume Designer .... Bobby Frederick Tilley
Lighting Designer .... Rui Rita
Sound Designer .... M L Dogg
Projection Designer .... Aaron Rhyne
Dramaturg .... Amy Levinson
Production Stage Manager .... Kyra Hansen
Assistant Stage Manager .... Michael Vitale
Casting Director .... Phyllis Schuringa

CHARACTERS

CHARLES DUFF (CHARLIE)
SUE RASPELL
JOHN EBBS
SCOTT ZOELLNER
RICK
CASEY

It is suggested that one actor play the following roles: TED;
BOB; NEIGHBOR; GREEK DINER HOST, CAR MECHANIC;
TIM BREWER, UNSHAVEN MAN *and (on video)* RON
KIRKPATRICK

characters on videos:
RON KIRKPATRICK
EMILY SALTER
DON SALTER
LYDIA SALTER
C N N REPORTER
20-SOMETHING PROTESTER
DISTINGUISHED PROFESSOR
ROCHESTER RESIDENT
OLDER WOMAN
CHINESE MAN
OLD TALMUDIC SCHOLAR
PRIEST
KORANIC SCHOLAR

characters just voice:
TED

MINISTER
CAR MECHANIC
LISA
LOCAL REPORTER
LOCAL REPORTER #2

The play's transitions should be handled with no more than a quiet light shift, the next scene's dialogue likely beginning as actors are moving.

Sets should be essentially nonexistent. Perhaps a news desk and a wall onto which images and video can be projected, but not much else. Locations such as CHARLIE's *apartment, his father's apartment,* CHARLIE's *office, the street…should be carved out by light, pockets of a vast landscape in which* CHARLIE *floats, looking for somewhere to land.*

Props should be minimal: A rocks glass here; maybe a cell phone there.

ACT ONE

(A T V news desk. Two anchors: CHARLES [CHARLIE] DUFF—*late 40s/early 50s, natural charisma but phoning it in at this point; and* SUE RASPELL, *30s, sexy if not for her uptightness and far too perfect hair. To the side is* JOHN EBBS, *30s, the jovial sportscaster.)*

CHARLIE: That does it for Channel 10 News tonight. Again, the top stories: A daring bank robbery at The First National Bank on 6th Street, carried out by two men wearing Incredible Hulk masks.

SUE: A proposed farm subsidy bill in Congress *may* affect local farmers.

CHARLIE: An eighty year-old farm-*hand* is arrested after repeatedly urinating on church facades.

SUE: *And*—Christmas comes early in Polish Town.
(Confused pause)
For Roger in the weather center, for John—

*(*JOHN *jovially waves good night—)*

SUE: —and from *all* of us here at Channel 10 News-—
(She looks to CHARLIE *for his ritual, polished sign-off—)*

CHARLIE: Have a safe and happy night.

*(*CHARLIE, SUE *and* JOHN *display toothy smiles as the closing music plays until the camera lights pop off and the studio lights come up to a general wash.)*

TED: *(O S) Clear!*

(CHARLIE *gathers his papers.*)

SUE: Good show, guys!

JOHN: I'll tell ya' —watching you two work is a luxury, every night.

SUE: *(To* CHARLIE*)* How come we ran the same segment on the robbery that we ran at six?

CHARLIE: *(Completely uninterested)* I don't know, Sue.

(—as they take off their body mics—)

SUE: *(To the production booth)* There was no update on the Hulk robbery, Ted?!

TED: *(O S. Via God mic)* Nothing that came in, Sue.

SUE: *(To* CHARLIE*)* Does the entire police force punch out at five?

CHARLIE: I doubt they had much to go on.

SUE: Go to the store that sells the Hulk masks and ask who bought two Hulk masks recently! Am I— I mean—?

JOHN: Hey Charlie, any chance of a drink?

CHARLIE: Not tonight, John—

JOHN: C'mon, the Razorsharks won!

CHARLIE: I don't really follow them—

JOHN: *They're the pride of Rochester!*—

CHARLIE: They can barely bounce a ball—

JOHN: But they *try!*—

CHARLIE: I'm sure they do—

JOHN: *So how can you not love 'em?!*

CHARLIE: *(Up to the booth)* I'll see you tomorrow, Ted.

TED: *(O S)* You got it, Charlie. Good show.

SUE: *(To* CHARLIE*)* Tomorrow we'll follow up on the farm fire in Livingston County?

CHARLIE: Up to you, Sue.

SUE: *(Shouting)* Ted, I wanna follow up on the cow story tomorrow!

TED: *(O S)* You got it, Sue.

SUE: *(To* CHARLIE*)* Three cows died, it's an important story.

JOHN: *(Faux grave) All* cow stories are important.

SUE: *(Fiery)* Have you ever *owned* a cow?

JOHN: Yes, Sue—*AND I FUCKIN' LOVE COWS!*

SUE: *(To* CHARLIE *re:* JOHN*)* Why is he like that? Does he have like, a—?

CHARLIE: He's just messin' with you, Sue.

SUE: Yes well there's "messing" and then there's sexual harassment.

JOHN: Oh *C'MON!*—

CHARLIE: John—

JOHN: *What?!*—

CHARLIE: You're yelling—

JOHN: *I KNOW!*

SUE: Charlie, I wanted to ask what you thought of my investigative piece.

CHARLIE: Ah—which one?

SUE: On the lack of programs at Five Points Prison. It was called "The Forgotten Ones"—?

CHARLIE: Oh right.

SUE: Scott liked it so I wanna propose a five-part series.

CHARLIE: Well remember that Scott has the intelligence of a guppy.

SUE: I'm trying to be serious.

CHARLIE: Sorry—yes, you should do it as a series.

SUE: You sure?

CHARLIE: The segment was great.

SUE: *(Delighted) Really?*

CHARLIE: It's the kinda stuff people don't think about.

SUE: You're humoring me.

CHARLIE: I'm not.

JOHN: He's definitely humoring you—

SUE: *(Ignoring)* Because that means a lot, considering your experience.

CHARLIE: Experience is just time; what you have is heart.

SUE: Thank you.
(A flattered smile)
I'll see you tomorrow.
(She leaves.)

JOHN: I actually *did* like her prison piece. Almost made me cry.

CHARLIE: I didn't really watch it.

JOHN: I love you, man—in a *sports* kinda way.

CHARLIE: Good to know.

JOHN: So the reason you don't wanna drink tonight is 'cause you're getting laid.

CHARLIE: Is it?

JOHN: Is it not?

CHARLIE: It might be.

JOHN: Seriously?

CHARLIE: No.

JOHN: You're lying.

CHARLIE: I'm not.

JOHN: You probably got some little Rock-U post-grad in "media communications" comin' over—

CHARLIE: That was one time—

JOHN: *It was last Friday!* You played me her voicemail! Why am *I* not getting laid?!

CHARLIE: Maybe talk with less volume. Women respond to that.

JOHN: *(Sotto voce)* Seriously?

CHARLIE: Have a good night, John.

JOHN: I'll admit there's a profound part of me that would like to cohabitate-in-a-bed with *Sue*.

CHARLIE: You're contractually prohibited.

JOHN: But it could raise our ratings.

CHARLIE: How?

JOHN: By greasing the hinges of her *emotional vault*.

CHARLIE: Fair enough.

JOHN: She's like a *cryogenic* Michele Bachmann.

CHARLIE: She's also married.

JOHN: True.

CHARLIE: See you tomorrow.
(He starts to go—)

JOHN: But Charlie?

(CHARLIE turns back)

JOHN: One of these days? A drink.

CHARLIE: Sure. One of these days.

JOHN: It's *pumpkin beer* season.

CHARLIE: (*Pause*) You know, John, the thing about getting laid is that it's generally fun. But at a certain age—

JOHN: It gets funner?

CHARLIE: No, it's always fun *while* you're doing it, it's just that afterwards, when you've shut the door and heard the elevator take her away, you sometimes turn back into your apartment…and it's suddenly *less* fun.

JOHN: 'Cause you gotta clean the sheets?

CHARLIE: No. You just sometimes wonder where the time went. For *both* of you.
(*Beat; small smile*)
Have a good one.

JOHN: …All right, man. See you tomorrow.

(JOHN *leaves;* CHARLIE *stands a moment, alone. He loosens his tie; in no hurry to leave the station. He closes his eyes, breathes, stands… Then:*)

TED: (*O S*) Charlie, there's a phone call for you on two.

CHARLIE: (*Stopping, puzzled*) For *me*?

TED: (*O S*) Yeah. It's your cousin, from Oregon? He says it's urgent.

(*—as lights shift—the sound of rain…and we are now at a funeral.*)

MINISTER: (*Voice*)
How calm; how beautiful comes on that stilly hour
When storms have gone; When warring winds have
   died away
And clouds and sea, beneath the dancing ray
Melt off and leave the land and sea
Floating in bright tranquility

(CHARLIE *looks up; he is alone on stage. The wind blows.*)

BOB: It was a nice service.

(—*as* CHARLIE *turns into his father's apartment. His cousin* BOB *is there in a baseball cap.*)

CHARLIE: Yeah. Simple. Low-key.

BOB: Just like the man. And I mean that in a good way. Your Dad was a…he was a good man, Charlie. And there's no question they loved him down at the bank. Took up a collection of six-hundred bucks for upkeep of the grave.

CHARLIE: They don't have to, I can—

BOB: They *want* to. I think he looked at them like family.

(CHARLIE *absorbs.*)

BOB: But of course he was always talking about his son Charlie. "The best anchor in Rochester." Probably loved you so much his heart gave out.

CHARLIE: I loved him too.

BOB: Of course you did.

CHARLIE: I hadn't gotten out here much the last couple years. Kept meaning to—

BOB: You can't blame yourself, Charlie. Oregon's a long way from Rochester and you're a busy guy. Two broadcasts a night. I don't know how you do it.

CHARLIE: I have a lotta free time during the day.

BOB: Well, you know what I mean.
(*Pause*)
If you want help packing some of this stuff up—

CHARLIE: I'm good.

BOB: Okay. But if you wanna grab a meal or something, just let me know. Carrie and the kids would love to see more of you—

CHARLIE: Will do.

BOB: …How's Lisa? I mean…

CHARLIE: She's fine. I don't see her much.

BOB: Good. And Ricky?

CHARLIE: Good. He's a…a good kid.

BOB: *(A nod…)* Okay then. Good to see you, cuz. Sorry for the circumstances.
(He shakes his hand, patting him gently on the shoulder, then leaves.)

(CHARLIE again alone. He looks around his dead father's apartment; its emptiness and lack of anything on which to grasp.)

(He perhaps finds a bottle of vodka with a bow around it; a glass; he pours a drink; takes a sip.)

(He closes his eyes…and sees a photograph.)

(—as on a wall is projected a photo of CHARLIE, around age 10, his dad standing next to him, arm proudly around his son…)

(The projection fades as he makes a phone call, though we perhaps don't see the phone.)

CHARLIE: Lisa, it's, Charlie; sorry to be calling so late. I know it's been a while. I'm actually calling from Oregon. …My father died. On Monday. Heart attack. My cousin Bob and I put together a little service this morning. Nothing much, which is why I didn't call you. But I probably should have. He, ah…he certainly did love you.
(Pause)
Anyway, I'm rambling. I hope you and Ricky are well. I'd love to see him, if he's ever…feeling up to that; and you too, of course.
(Pause)
Okay. Bye.

(CHARLIE stands alone—as lights fade…)

(—*and the video pops on with a giant image of* RON KIRKPATRICK, *the peppy and energetic Channel 10 reporter standing outside a bowling alley.)*

RON: —and so, in his own special way, Jerry Basker makes a *very big* difference in the bowling alleys of Rochester. For Channel 10 News, this is Ron Kirkpatrick!

(—*as the video fades and lights shift to the anchor desk, where* CHARLIE *has taken his place next to* SUE *and* JOHN, *as we hear.)*

SUE: Thanks, Ron.
(To CHARLIE*)*
Inspirational stuff.

CHARLIE: Sure is.

JOHN: It's all about making a difference.

(As SUE *starts to speak:)*

JOHN: And what a great name "Basker" is.

*(*SUE *looks at* JOHN *with annoyance, then:)*

SUE: That does it for Channel 10 tonight. Again our top story: The cow death toll rises following the devastating farm fire in Livingston County.

CHARLIE: And the Rochester Philharmonic Orchestra boosts its number of subscribers for the second year in a row.

SUE: *(Happy about the orchestra)* For Roger in the weather center, for John—

*(*JOHN *jovially waves good night—)*

SUE: —and from *all* of us here at Channel 10 News-—
(She looks to CHARLIE *for his usual sign off.)*

CHARLIE: Have a safe and happy
(He stops. And when he speaks again, it is a touch slower and more genuine than usual.)

Before we sign off, I'd like to, on a personal note, to…
to send out a prayer to my recently departed father,
Gene Duff.
(Slightly formal; eyes closed)
To wherever your soul might be tonight, Dad, may
it be near God, and may you be resting in peace. I'm
sorry that I wasn't there for you more. I love you.
(Opening his eyes, looking up)
Have a safe and happy night.

*(Closing music begins, studio lights dim and they're off
air—)*

TED: *(O S) Clear!*

*(JOHN and SUE are staring at CHARLIE in disbelief. He
briefly looks back, then stands and takes off his mic.)*

JOHN: Wow.

SUE: What on *earth* did you just do?

CHARLIE: Just wanted to say something about my Dad,
Sue.

SUE: *Why?*

CHARLIE: Because he died. That's why I wasn't here for
a few days—

SUE: I realize that, and I'm sorry, but you can't just…
pray.

CHARLIE: I know. But I guess I did.

JOHN: Dude, you do realize that Zoellner's gonna
screw you a new asshole. Like twist a corkscrew into a
previously uninfiltrated crevice—

SUE: It's a *news show*, Charlie!—

JOHN: Not to mention *Roger* over in the Weather Center
feeling left out and abandoned.

CHARLIE: There's no such thing as the Weather Center,
John, it's a renovated closet in the basement.

JOHN: Tell that to fucking *Roger!*

CHARLIE: *(To the booth)* I'll see you tomorrow, Ted.

TED: *(O S)* Ah, I *guess.*

(CHARLIE *turns and nods good night to* JOHN *and* SUE, *then turns away*—)

(—*into new light, where he stands a moment, checking in with what he just did, and felt…as:*)

(*Lights shift to the next day*—)

JOHN: High school hoops season preview. Gonna be a *big* year.

(CHARLIE *steps into his office at the T V station, where John awaits*—)

CHARLIE: *Nice.*

JOHN: Did Zoellner fire you yet?

CHARLIE: He left voicemails.

JOHN: You didn't call him back?

CHARLIE: *(A shake of the head)* It was eleven-thirty at night, we're third in the ratings, there were twenty-two people watching total.

JOHN: I dunno, man, I was just upstairs with Ted and he said the switchboard lit up the second we went off-air.

CHARLIE: "Switchboard"?

JOHN: You know what I mean, Chuckles. Our Facebook page got like *ten thousand hits*, plus phone calls, emails, *SnapChat-shit.*

CHARLIE: All I did was mention my Dad—

JOHN: You *prayed*, dude!—

CHARLIE: *Everyone* prays.

JOHN: May-be—

CHARLIE: So why're they on our Facebook page?

JOHN: Because the world is full of fuck-dunces.

(—as SUE *walks by, all business, not looking up.*)

CHARLIE: Hi, Sue.

SUE: Hi.
(Pause)
Have you looked at the breakdown?

CHARLIE: I just got in.

SUE: Ted wants to lead with the politically disoriented turkey hunter.

CHARLIE: Fine with me.

SUE: Well I don't *care* what the turkey hunter thinks about health care—

CHARLIE: So then what do you want instead?

SUE: The Haskell scandal. It's a no-brainer.

CHARLIE: Sounds great.

SUE: I'll let him know.
(She shuffles papers, not looking up…)
I understand that something happened to you last night…
(Still not looking up)
But I would prefer that it never happen again. You wanna pray, go be a priest.

CHARLIE: Not sure I'm cut out for it.

SUE: *(Finally looking up)* Did Zoellner reach you?

CHARLIE: He's at a network meeting in New York.

JOHN: What'd he say on your voicemail?

CHARLIE: That if I'd prayed at *six* I'd be out of a job.

JOHN: *Spoken like a douche!*

SUE: *(Point blank, to* CHARLIE*)* Are you even *religious*? Because it could quite frankly be considered offensive to *honestly* religious people for you to be bandying about God's name over the airwaves like—

CHARLIE: —I wouldn't say I was "bandying it about"—

SUE: —*you know what I mean.*
(Re: her papers)
Why on earth does Ron Kirkpatrick think that *anyone in their right mind* cares about what the turkey hunter thinks?!

CHARLIE: Sue?

SUE: What?

CHARLIE: The turkeys care.

*(*SUE *looks at* CHARLIE*, momentarily perplexed. Then turns to go.)*

SUE: I'll be in my office.

*(*SUE *leaves. Beat)*

JOHN: I think she likes you.
(No response)
Hey Charlie?

*(*CHARLIE *looks up)*

JOHN: Over 10-thousand hits. We usually get about ten.

(—as lights shift and CHARLIE *and* JOHN *take their place at the anchor desk, the video now showing footage of an ice skating rink full of grown men wearing nothing but skates and loin clothes.)*

RON KIRKPATRICK: *(O S)* From the Irondiquoit Nude Cherry Ball Charitable Ice Dance, I'm Ron Kirkpatrick for Channel 10 News! Back to Charles and Sue.

(—as the video fades and the anchors wrap up with banter.)

SUE: Boy, I wouldn't want to be a belle at that ball.

JOHN: Balls like that can get mighty cold.

SUE: (*Trying not to react*) Okay then, that wraps it up for Channel 10 at six. The stories we'll be following throughout tomorrow: *Snow* might be headed our way for Halloween.

CHARLIE: The downtown Ramada celebrates its twenty-fifth year of existence.

SUE: And the next segment in my investigative series on prison reform at Five Points Correctional Facility.

(CHARLIE *looks at her*)

SUE: For Roger in the weather center, for John—

(JOHN *jovially waves good night*—)

SUE: —and from *all* of us here at Channel 10 News-— (*She turns to* CHARLIE *for his usual sign-off*—)

CHARLIE: Before signing off I'd like to thank those of you who expressed your kind wishes for the passing of my father.
(*Genuine*)
Your comments and emails, which I read this afternoon, gave me great solace.
(*Pause*)
So on that note, I'd like to send out a prayer to *everyone* who's lost someone recently.
(*Head bowed*)
That they might keep in mind that if we can't know *why*, we should at least have faith that the *absence* of our loved ones might, in some unexpected way…allow us to better love the people still *in* our lives.
(*Pause; looking up*)
Good night.

(*End music swells as they go off air.*)

TED: (*O S*) Clear!

CHARLIE: Stop staring at me, Sue.

SUE: I just don't think you can *do* that.

JOHN: You're fucking crazy, dude—in a *good* way—

SUE: You're gonna get yourself *fired*.

CHARLIE: Worse things have happened.

SUE: *(To* JOHN, *snapping)* And why the *hell* are you talking about *cold balls*!?

JOHN: They're just balls, Sue.

TED: *(O S)* Charlie, Scott wants to talk to you on set.

CHARLIE: Right now?

TED: *(O S)* He's on his way down.

*(*SCOTT ZOELLNER *enters. He's younger than* CHARLIE *but more powerful; a rising star at the network, and a prick who loves to act humble.)*

ZOELLNER: Charlie—

CHARLIE: Scott.

JOHN: How was New York, Mr Zoellner?—

ZOELLNER: *John—*

JOHN: Sorry.

ZOELLNER: *(To* CHARLIE; *formal; "nice")* Charles, I'm sorry your father died, I truly am.

CHARLIE: Thank you.

ZOELLNER: I'm sure he was a very noble man.

*(*CHARLIE *waits.)*

ZOELLNER: Charles, do you *believe* in God?
(Re: the others)
I'm sorry, should we do this in private?

CHARLIE: It's okay.

ZOELLNER: *(To* JOHN *and* SUE) If you have to go—

JOHN: There's actually a long history of sports and religion intermingling on a deeply *holistic* level, so I should probably stay.

SUE: I'll stay.

(ZOELLNER returns his look to CHARLIE.)

CHARLIE: ...I guess I've always been suspicious.

ZOELLNER: Of—?

CHARLIE: Some sort of...force. To be reckoned with.

ZOELLNER: And that force is God?

JOHN: Well it's not Mike Huckabee—

ZOELLNER: I need you to zip it, sports-man.
(To CHARLIE)
This is gonna sound corny, Charles—

CHARLIE: Charlie—

ZOELLNER: Charlie—it's gonna sound corny, but when it comes to this broadcast, *I'm* the higher force, meaning there's really *no room* for God; certainly not an *overt* God. Innate? Private? —Go for it. *On-air credit?* —Can't have it—not allowed—

CHARLIE: Right—

ZOELLNER: You're a great anchor and I consider myself lucky to have you around. Most guys with your talent seek out the bigger markets.

CHARLIE: Well I actually *did*—

ZOELLNER: Well I'm glad it never worked out; for *our* sake. You're a superstar *here.* But do me a favor and don't pray on my program.

JOHN: You *have* said you want a more intimate viewer relationship.

ZOELLNER: John—intimacy is making a joke about the unpredictability of weather. Praying for your dead father is unsettling and creepy—
(To CHARLIE*)*
—not creepy specific to your father—

CHARLIE: I got you—

ZOELLNER: I'm not speaking in tongues here, am I? You get what I'm saying. We have Jews and Muslims who watch this program.

JOHN: Really?—

ZOELLNER: A couple, maybe *three.*

SUE: He wasn't speaking to a specific denomination, Scott.

ZOELLNER· I know that, *Sue,* but Charlie doesn't really *look* Arab or Jewish—

JOHN: Or *neo-Quaker*—

ZOELLNER: *I swear to God, John!*—

JOHN: Sorry.

ZOELLNER: *(Calmer—to* CHARLIE*)* I was in New York today and thankfully the network bigwigs hadn't caught wind of last night's little ecclesiastical shout-out, but now there's a good chance they *will* and *I'll* be the one who has to deal, so don't pray again—
(Suddenly very serious)
—or I'll be forced to terminate you starting immediately. We're a news show, Charlie, providing untarnished, unslanted, *uninflected* information. We don't provide "solace," and given the length of your experience you should know that better than anyone in this fucking room.
(Pause)
You didn't feel like calling me back today?

CHARLIE: I knew you were traveling.

ZOELLNER: Right. Call me back next time, Charles.
(He turns to go)
All right. *Good talk!*

*(ZOELLNER leaves, having put a definite chill in the air.
Pause)*

JOHN: That guy brings new meaning to the term "Blow
me."
(Hand out to CHARLIE)
I'll see you at eleven?

*(CHARLIE nods and shakes his hand. JOHN leaves. SUE
gathers her papers…but after a moment turns to CHARLIE.)*

SUE: It's about compartmentalization.

CHARLIE: What is?

SUE: Everything. God; your job; your personal life.
They need to be *separate*. My son? Luke? How do you
think I deal with that?

CHARLIE: What do you mean?

SUE: *(Realizing he's forgotten)* He's autistic, Charlie. He's
on the autistic spectrum.

CHARLIE: I had no idea.

SUE: Yes you did. We've talked about it—

CHARLIE: Oh—right—I'm so sorry—

SUE: It doesn't matter. I specifically try not to discuss
it because I refuse to be defined by it. Yes it's a never-
ceasing part of my life, but if I walked in here everyday
with a T-shirt saying "My son is autistic", I would
never reach fulfillment as a serious news journalist.

CHARLIE: I understand—

SUE: Certain things don't mix.
(Pause; softer)

The work we do here is good.

CHARLIE: You've already given the pep talk, Sue—

SUE: But not the peppy part. Because I can see how the work might not always seem *"vital"*. But people do watch; what we do does makes a difference.

CHARLIE: You're right.
(Honest)
Thank you.

(—lights shift CHARLIE *steps toward his apartment. A* NEIGHBOR *approaches.)*

NEIGHBOR: Hi—sorry—-Charles Duff, right?

CHARLIE: Yes.

NEIGHBOR: I don't mean to bother you, I live down the hall; we sometimes pass.

CHARLIE: Oh. Right.

NEIGHBOR: I saw your broadcast earlier, when you said the prayer for people who have, you know, lost someone.

CHARLIE: Oh, okay.

NEIGHBOR: I lost my wife a couple years ago. Brain tumor, outta the blue; go figure.

CHARLIE: ...God must've needed another angel.

NEIGHBOR: Yeah, but, thing is, I'm not really a big believer in that one. Anyway—
(He can't finish.)

CHARLIE: I'm sorry. About your wife.

NEIGHBOR: *(A small nod...)* I guess I just wanted to say thanks. It's a fine line between moving on and denial. And you sorta made me check in. With stuff that I hadn't been checking in with. Gave she and I a little.... connection, I guess. Anyway—thanks.

(NEIGHBOR *extends his hand.* CHARLIE *shakes it.*)

NEIGHBOR: Have a good night.

(CHARLIE *watches as* NEIGHBOR *moves on. He then steps into his apartment; a lovely view of the twinkling Rochester skyline.*)

(*He takes off his jacket and tie, perhaps fixes a drink, methodical and precise. Then, unsure what to do, he makes a phone call… [Again, we may not need to see an actual phone.]*)

CHARLIE: Ricky, it's your Dad. How are you, buddy? I was gonna call your Mom again but then I thought I'd just call direct, which I hope's okay. I know it's been awhile since we've spoken and that that's how you… want it to be, but I was hoping we could get together and maybe talk about…finding a way to talk again. Maybe I take you to lunch sometime?
(*Pause*)
Okay. Call me. …Bye.
(*He hangs up, feeling awkward. He stands alone, watching the sparkling lights out his window…*)

(—*as lights shift back to the T V station, where* JOHN *is at* CHARLIE'*s dressing room door:*)

JOHN: You got a sec'?

CHARLIE: Sure.

JOHN: You checked in with Ted today?

CHARLIE: Haven't been down there yet.

JOHN: (*A nod; beat*) You know what a trending tweet is, right? A fuckin' *tweet that trends*?

CHARLIE: Yeah, I know what a trending tweet is.

JOHN: Because we all know *Joe-the-intern* manages your Tweets.

CHARLIE: I still know what one is.

JOHN: Good, because our station's Twitter got twelve thousand twenty-four *re-tweets* last night, which is a fuckin' trend. It's nuts. Seems that pretty much *every single one* of our viewers has lost someone in recent years and were thus "immensely moved" by your prayer for all the "lost souls".

(CHARLIE *nods...*)

JOHN: You see those folks out in the parking lot?
(Looking out a window to below)
I don't know how many were there when you got here but it's up to about fifty now. Some with signs.

CHARLIE: Saying what?

JOHN: "In Duff We Trust." "God loves you, Charles." "Charlie, I want you inside me."

(Off CHARLIE's *look:)*

JOHN: No, but there is a chick out there who's *smokin'*. I mean you know how sometimes very evangelical women are just *totally tasty* in that sort of reverent, ecstatic, *orgasmic* kinda way? To the point where their ta-ti-ta's are fundamentally *pointy and...spire-like?* — Perhaps emblematic of their trust in a higher being? Sort of an anti-gravitational...*attention*?

(CHARLIE *doesn't respond.*)

JOHN: Granted there was also some negative stuff, like a post labeling you "Satanic Butt Nibbler". But mostly they love you, man; love ya' like a rock.

CHARLIE: ...Did you know that Sue has an autistic son?

JOHN: Ah—ya.

CHARLIE: Did *I* know that?

JOHN: You should've.

CHARLIE: She doesn't talk about it a lot.

JOHN: I know but it completely dominates her life. I also have a hunch it's completely screwing up her marriage.

CHARLIE: With James?

JOHN: *Yes—with James.* She doesn't have seventeen husbands, Charlie, her husband's name is James.

(CHARLIE *nods*)

JOHN: Why?

CHARLIE: I guess I just…I missed that. Or forgot; at some point; that that's an issue in her life.

JOHN: It's definitely an issue.
(*Beat*)
You gonna pray tonight?

CHARLIE: No.

(—*as lights shift and the video shows a highly uncoordinated baby giraffe stumbling as its mother looks on.*)

RON: *(O S)* And so as you can see, baby giraffe and mother are doing *just fine* thank you!

(—*as* RON, *perfectly blow-dried hair, tip-toes into the frame.*)

RON: —and if all goes well, young Cornelius will be around for many years to come. From the Rochester Zoo, this is Ron Kirkpatrick for Channel 10 News!

(—*as the video fades and the anchors, now seated, wrap up with banter.*)

SUE: What a cutie, poor thing can't even stand.

CHARLIE: *(Off teleprompter)* But I'm sure he'll have some "tall" tales to tell some day.

JOHN: Let's hope he learns how to *walk* first! And that his mother doesn't keep him on too tight a leash. We all know how suffocating *that* can be.

SUE: That's it for Channel 10 News tonight. Once again, today's top stories: Republican legislators pass an ambitious farm subsidy bill.

(The video now shows an enlarged photo of a nine year-old girl with the word "MISSING" across it—)

CHARLIE: And a ransom note today for eleven year-old Emily Salter, who went missing last night from a Pittsford mall. Her abductors are demanding two million dollars for her release.

SUE: For Roger in the weather center, for John, and for *all* of us in the Channel 10 newsroom—

CHARLIE: I would like to put forth a prayer; that the kidnappers might…look within themselves, to somewhere in their hearts—beneath the greed, the anger, whatever it is that's driving their behavior, and that they might find something more…*human*, down there, which will encourage them to do what is right; and return this young girl to her parents.
(He lowers his head a moment… and then looks back up)
Thank you. Have a safe and happy night.

(Music up, cameras off.)

TED: *(O S) Clear!*

JOHN: I'm staying for this one!

SUE: *(Exiting)* I'm not.

CHARLIE: It's really not gonna be that exciting—

TED: *(O S)* Charlie, Scott would like to speak to you.

CHARLIE: Here or in his office?

TED: *(O S)* Umm—I'm not sure—

(ZOELLNER enters, enraged—)

ZOELLNER: What the fuck is your prepubescent problem, Duff?

CHARLIE: It wasn't something I planned.

ZOELLNER: Oh—should I grab my balls for joy? Did I not ask politely?—

CHARLIE: You did—

ZOELLNER: It is just *so* wrong on so many levels—
(Counting them off)
Journalistic integrity, religious pluralism, F C C regulation, The League of Benevolent Atheists, I mean—

CHARLIE: Scott—

ZOELLNER: What?!

CHARLIE: Everyone watching wants that girl to be released!—

ZOELLNER: *Irrelevant!*—

CHARLIE: Why is praying for something that everyone wants irrelevant?—

ZOELLNER: You're missing the point!—

CHARLIE: It's no different than editorial commentary—

ZOELLNER: It's different because you're invoking *God*, you pious fuck! I'm trying to run an impartial news program, not The Billy Graham Theological Fireside Chat!

CHARLIE: I'm not—

ZOELLNER: *Fuck you!*

CHARLIE: Fine.

ZOELLNER: My job, Charlie, is to fight the good fight. To not succumb to the temptation of sentimentally catering to the masses. Central to the *American Experiment* is objective coverage and dissemination of the events that take place in our society. That is an unambiguous and unimpeachable *right* of the human beings who have signed the social contract of this country—whether they actually *want* it or not!

JOHN: Yeah but that's not really how it works anymore—

ZOELLNER: *Go cover girls softball, John!*
(To CHARLIE*)*
I may be a dick but I'm right about this.
(And then)
You're indefinitely suspended, pending a review; most likely to result in termination. Our lawyers will be in contact.

*(*ZOELLNER *leaves. Beat)*

JOHN: …Wanna grab a drink?

CHARLIE: Not tonight.

*(*CHARLIE *leaves…as lights shift—)*

(—and he steps into his apartment. He hears messages. Snow has begun to fall.)

CAR MECHANIC: *(O S. Thick Irish brogue)* Charles, this is Aiden down at Mcdonough Auto Repair. Hope I'm not bothering you, but I saw your appeal on the news earlier and wanted to reach out and commend you. First time I've felt moved by the spirit in a very long while. And this from a man who's thrown a large number of bricks through many a' church window. So just wanted to put that out there. Cheers.

*(*CHARLIE *maybe smiles a bit. And then:)*

LISA: *(O S)* Hey Charlie, it's Lisa. I'm so, so sorry about your Dad. I really am. He was…well—he was a *lovely* man.

(As LISA *continues, we are simply watching* CHARLIE, *his face absorbing every word. He is alone on a practically bare stage, listening.)*

LISA: *(O S)* So—thanks for the message. Obviously it would've been nice to have been out there for the service, but…I understand it was probably last minute. *(Reverting to more neutral)*
Rick told me you called him too. Which I'm not sure how he took, seeing as he's pretty tight-lipped when it comes to the subject of…*you.* So you'll have to handle that one on your own for awhile.
(Pause)
Anyway, hope all else is well on your end. Thanks again for the call. Bye.

(CHARLIE absorbs. The snow has picked up; it's gorgeous. He sips his drink. Stillness but for the snow. And then— sound of a phone ring…)

CHARLIE: Hello?…What?…*Really?*

(The video snaps to life with an image of RON standing outside a Walmart.)

RON: And so it is that at just noon yesterday the kidnappers were demanding two million dollars for the release of young Emily Salter, and a mere *eleven* hours later she's dropped off in this Wal-Mart parking lot—*for free.*

(Footage now shows 11 year-old EMILY being walked out of a police station surrounded by police and her parents.)

RON: *(V O)* Channel 10 was granted an exclusive interview with Emily and her parents as they returned to their Fairport home.

(Video shows RON on the lawn of a large suburban house holding a mic for EMILY and her parents, DON and LYDIA SALTER. Beneath DON is the subtitle, "Emily's father, President and CEO of Salter Furniture.")

DON SALTER: I had actually met with my banker because we were ready to pay the ransom. And then we got the call from the police…and didn't believe it. We thought it was some kind of joke.

(*As the camera widens to show* LYDIA, *we also see young* EMILY, *standing quietly between her clinging parents, looking glassy-eyed and shell-shocked.*)

LYDIA SALTER: We just thank God; or maybe I should say we thank Charles Duff. We didn't think it would turn out this way. We are just so, *so* thankful. It's like a miracle.

(*Video on* RON *again in the parking lot.*)

RON: From the Walmart in Fairport, this is Ron Kirkpatrick for Channel 10 News.

(*Video fades as lights rise on* CHARLIE *in his dressing room drinking a Snapple and being talked at by* JOHN—)

JOHN: It's *deep*, man. It's like…it's fucking *deeeep*.

CHARLIE: Could be a coincidence.

JOHN: Could be—*or* it could be a *meaningful* coincidence. Synchronicity. I'm talking Jung, I'm talking cosmic convergence, I'm talking they heard your prayer even if they didn't *hear* your prayer.

CHARLIE: Maybe they just heard my prayer.

JOHN: *Well then they fuckin' heard your prayer! Your shit works!*

(SUE *is there. Pause*)

CHARLIE: Hi, Sue.

SUE: What you did last night was wrong.
(*Pause*)
But thank you for doing it.

(SUE *hugs* CHARLIE…*then starts to leave*—)

CHARLIE: Sue?

(SUE *turns back.*)

CHARLIE: You okay?

SUE: Yes.

(She regards him; smiles, and leaves.)

JOHN: Dude, she hasn't hugged anyone in like fourteen years.

(Pause)

Why are you even *here*? I thought you were suspended.

CHARLIE: Zoellner asked to see me.

JOHN: That guy's a fucking dickless *carnival*; total fucking monkey's sphincter.

(Pause)

Should I not curse so much around you?

CHARLIE: Up to you.

JOHN: …That crowd out there quadrupled over night.

CHARLIE: They should get jobs.

JOHN: They *have* jobs. They're professional *devotees*. People are dropping off flowers, fruit, those little Mother Teresa dolls that don't tip no matter how hard you push.

(Pause)

Roger says he's gonna get you praying for the accu-forecast.

(No response)

Ted showed me a blog dubbing you "Jesus of Rochester". It had your headshot photoshopped with a beard, dreadlocks, and riding a mule wearing Tommy Hilfiger underwear. And don't ask how many tweets.

CHARLIE: I won't.

JOHN: Well you should because this time they're *requests*!

CHARLIE: For what?

JOHN: For *prayer*, man! Everything from "Please pray that my epileptic dog not drool on the couch," to "Please mend my daughter's anti-Biblical ways." There was even a woman wanting you to pray to have her *cervical area* enlarged.

CHARLIE: John—maybe lay off the *overt* sexism?

JOHN: *I'm sorry— It's a problem!*

(CHARLIE *and* JOHN *are now distracted by* ZOELLNER, *who is at the door watching* CHARLIE *with a poker face.*)

CHARLIE: …Hi, Scott.

ZOELLNER: Hi.

JOHN: Do you want me to leave?

ZOELLNER: Doesn't matter.

JOHN: Awesome.

(JOHN *makes himself comfortable as* ZOELLNER *continues to laser* CHARLIE *with his stare….. And then:*)

ZOELLNER: Here's the deal: I fucking hate religion. Okay? I look at the stars, I think about fireballs, not "God". Most of the guys who started these "big religions" *also* thought the sun rotated around the earth and that retarded kids were the devil's work. You ask me, religion is the neglected and deluded step-child of *logic and reason.* Thus *I* think what you're doing is technically some sorta crime against humanity.
(Pause)
But—I'm also not an idiot. The power of prayer is deep and the power of ratings profound. The numbers for our show—and I use the word "show" here not by accident because we are a show, we are *showmen, and "women"*, presenting nothing short of *spectacle.* The numbers for our *show* have dramatically spiked since you transformed the anchor desk into a pulpit.
(Pause; leaning in)

So here's what I'm gonna do: I'm not gonna say *anything* to you right now, other than what I'm saying, which is nothing.

CHARLIE: Okay.

ZOELLNER: Your suspension is lifted until I hear otherwise from the network. We're gonna let this play out in a smart, innocent, godly way.

CHARLIE: You want me to keep working?

ZOELLNER: I want you to keep working.

CHARLIE: Am I supposed to—

ZOELLNER: It's up to you. You seem to be working from your instincts on this—A K A out your *ass*—so you should probably just keep doing that until someone tells us not to. Call it like you see it, do what feels right, don't get caught *diddling* little boys.

JOHN: What about me?

ZOELLNER: *(Exiting)* Shave the pubic hair off your face.

(—as lights shift…and CHARLIE *is alone inside the entrance of a diner. He looks at his watch, looks around…)*

(After several moments RICK, *his 16 year-old son, arrives. The kid is guarded and monosyllabic, until he's not.)*

CHARLIE: Hey, buddy.

RICK: Hey.

CHARLIE: Jesus you're tall.

*(*RICK *maybe nods)*

CHARLIE: You look great.

(Not even a nod)

CHARLIE: I was stupid to pick this place, it's packed so…the guy said it might be a couple minutes.
(Pause)
Thanks for meeting me.

RICK: Sure.

CHARLIE: What were you up to today?

RICK: It's a Saturday.

CHARLIE: I know, so—what were you up to? Basketball practice?

RICK: I'm not on the team.

CHARLIE: Why?

RICK: Didn't wanna play J V.

CHARLIE: But, you're in 10th grade, isn't that *normal* for a—?

RICK: I just didn't wanna play.

(CHARLIE *nods.*)

RICK: *(Beat)* I'm in a band but I don't wanna talk about it.

CHARLIE: Okay. Cool.
(Pause)
Listen, Ricky—

RICK: It's actually Rick.

CHARLIE: What?—

RICK: Not Ricky. Rick.

CHARLIE: Okay. ...Is that—?

RICK: It's shorter.

CHARLIE: Right.
(He nods...)
I was actually playing basketball for awhile this fall.
Some of my camera guys rent out the gym at Nichols on Sunday mornings, but then my knee started hurting.

RICK: Maybe you should pray for it.

CHARLIE: What? —Oh, I didn't know you'd been—

RICK: I haven't. Mom told me.

CHARLIE: I'm surprised it's not on YouTube; not that it deserves—

RICK: It *is* on YouTube.

CHARLIE: Really?

RICK: You didn't know that?

CHARLIE: No.

(RICK *stares at* CHARLIE.)

CHARLIE: Well, yeah, I heard some of the guys at work. *(Pause)*
So you *never* watch the broadcast?

RICK: I turn it on for sports.

CHARLIE: Oh—you like John Ebbs?

RICK: Yeah, the guy's totally demented.

CHARLIE: Yeah—

RICK: He's cool.

(…*A sycophantic* GREEK DINER HOST *walks by*.)

DINER HOST: Mr Duff, I'm so sorry, can you wait 4 more minutes?

CHARLIE: Of course—

DINER HOST: There's an annoying woman, massively annoying and she won't leave—see her there?—

CHARLIE: Yeah—

DINER HOST: She's fucking annoying this woman, but hopefully she'll leave soon. You won't abandon us, will you?

CHARLIE: No—

DINER HOST: *Thank* you, Mr Duff! *You are the man!* You are *the man*, Mr Duff!

(The DINER HOST *leaves. Beat)*

CHARLIE: Anyway. Yeah—I think the prayers should probably be a bit more selfless than for my knee.

RICK: Why?

CHARLIE: ...Because it's good to be selfless? And I probably haven't done enough of that in my life.

*(*RICK *just stares at* CHARLIE.*)*

CHARLIE: Mom told you about Grandpa?

*(*RICK *nods. Pause)*

RICK: Yeah. I'm really sorry.

CHARLIE: Thanks.

(Pause)

...I remember when you were born. My Dad came out to visit and he couldn't stop staring at you with this, this humongous smile on his face. And he just kept saying, "He's a keeper, Charlie. This kid's a true keeper."

(Pause)

He used to call you "The best damn kid in the kid store."

(Beat. RICK *gives* CHARLIE *very little.)*

CHARLIE: Look, Ricky, I know what you're gonna say—

RICK: No you don't—

CHARLIE: I know what you *could* say right now and I'd probably say it too if I were in your shoes—

RICK: But you're not—

CHARLIE: No I'm not, but the *point* is—well, you've *made* your point. You asked me to butt outta your life and I've pretty much honored that for two years now, so I think it's fair for me to expect some sort of, you know, second chance—

RICK: Can I ask you something?

CHARLIE: Yes.

RICK: What are you thinking our relationship is gonna be right now? Are you expecting that we're gonna be "best buds" again?

CHARLIE: No—

RICK: Are you looking for someone to chat on the phone with about girls?—

CHARLIE: Look, Ricky—

RICK: *Rick.*

CHARLIE: …Sorry. Rick. I, ah, I would like for us to—

RICK: Can I interrupt?

(CHARLIE *waits.*)

RICK: You may have certain people falling for your little *saint* routine but you shouldn't count on *me* for that. Because I know what you are. I know what you did to Mom, I know how much you cheated, I know how much lied, I know how much you deeply hurt her feelings on a regular fucking basis—and so I know how totally hypocritical it is for you to be on T V each night pretending to be some sort of "holy and haunted *prophet*". I *know* all that, and I'm not falling for it.

CHARLIE: …You know about the affairs?

RICK: I'm not an idiot.

CHARLIE: Mom told you?

RICK: Oh—what—now you're gonna blame *Mom* for answering me honestly about why you guys got divorced? —Is that how you're gonna play this?—

CHARLIE: I'm just asking—

RICK: *Yes, she told me;* I'm sixteen years old and I asked her and she decided that truthfulness was the right approach, shocking as that might sound to you.

CHARLIE: ...I'm not asking you to fall for anything—

RICK: I actually *did* go on YouTube.

CHARLIE: ...What'd you see?

RICK: The one where you prayed for the capsized fishing boat.
(And then, deadpan)
Totally heartbreaking.

CHARLIE: You don't think something good came out of it?

RICK: They plucked some fat guys out of a lake.
(And then)
If you're gonna pray for something, pray for that prison that your co-anchor keeps talking about.

CHARLIE: ...So you *have* watched more than just sports.

RICK: Mom had it on at dinner.

(CHARLIE nods; they stand... Then:)

RICK: I actually gotta be somewhere.

CHARLIE: What are you talking about?—

RICK: I forgot I had a thing—

CHARLIE: Ricky—

RICK: It's fucking *Rick*, not Ricky!

CHARLIE: Rick—I'm sorry—but listen: I would like to find a way back in.

RICK: Why?

CHARLIE: Because I miss you.

RICK: *(Beat)* Why are you praying on T V?

CHARLIE: I don't know.

(Beat; RICK *extends his hand—)*

RICK: Yeah so I gotta go. Good to see you.

*(*CHARLIE *looks at* RICK's *hand...and shakes it.* RICK *turns and leaves.)*

(—as lights shift—)

(—to CHARLIE's *dressing room, where* JOHN *is working a smart phone—)*

JOHN: Dude: Brilliant move.

CHARLIE: What?

JOHN: Your prayer for Five Points Prison last night?— set off a tidal wave of donations.

CHARLIE: For—?

JOHN: More programs, longer visiting hours, better food. Sue's gonna have a Happy Attack. I mean— *thirty-six thousand in less than a day.*

CHARLIE: Really?

JOHN: This keeps up, they'll end up getting Guy Fieri to cook these guys dinner each night.

CHARLIE: I'm not sure Guy Fieri constitutes prison reform.

JOHN: Charlie, prisoners *riot* over food.

CHARLIE: Is that right?

JOHN: I also wouldn't put it past the people of Rochester to start sending in mass platters of lasagna. Because when it comes to food, there is no community on *earth* that's gonna bake more lasagna. We're like the lasagna capitol of upper-northern-western upstate New York!
(Looking up from phone)
I mean, Sue's reports are good. That one with the nineteen year-old kid who's in for fifty years? The one

who just sat there and stared at the camera? He just
looked so fucking...
(A long and kinda scary pause...)
...lost. Just shut away and forgotten. And then *you* say
a prayer—and suddenly we remember.
(And then, amped back up)
You're fucking *uniting* people, dude. And it's not like
Facebook where it's like, "Oh hey Billy, it's sunny
here in China". It's more like, "Hey, my brother, you
are my fellow human being and I love you and I'm
going to *care for you* and *that's* what gives my life some
meaning."
(Genuine)
It's fuckin' *visceral*, man.

CHARLIE: ...Maybe.

JOHN: *(Beat...)* Hey Charlie?

(Beat; CHARLIE looks up)

JOHN: I'm not a happy person.

(CHARLIE waits for the punch line, but there isn't one.)

CHARLIE: What do you mean?

JOHN: I'm on so many antidepressants I can barely take
a shit.

CHARLIE: I didn't know that.

JOHN: That I can't take a shit?

CHARLIE: ...You don't *seem*...to be a depressed person,
John.

JOHN: Yeah. I know. I make jokes for fifteen hours
straight, then go home and cry. Literally; I cry myself
to sleep six nights outta seven. That's why I'm always
trying to get you to go for a drink, you fuck.
(Pause)

You really think I was taking a vacation last year? For two weeks—during the N B A *finals*?

CHARLIE: But you're like, jovial whenever I see you.

JOHN: That's why they call it *manic*, dipshit.

CHARLIE: I'm sorry. I didn't know.

JOHN: It's not usually my lead story.

CHARLIE: I know, but I've known you for six years.

JOHN: I guess we weren't really feeling the "visceral connective tissue." And I'm not trying to make you feel bad, *at all*. The reason I'm telling you is 'cause I actually *do* feel…connected, these days, because of what you're doing. It's made me feel less shitty. About how shitty I feel.

CHARLIE: Why?

JOHN: …I don't know.

CHARLIE: …Thank you for telling me. It means a lot.

JOHN: You don't have to say that.

CHARLIE: I know. But it's true.

(Pause)

JOHN: You should go visit that prison.

CHARLIE: …I no longer do field work, John.

JOHN: Why not?

CHARLIE: You want me to go visit prisoners?

JOHN: You can't just pray in a vacuum.

CHARLIE: It can if it works.

JOHN: Be serious. I think you should go.

CHARLIE: It's not what I do.

JOHN: It should be.
(And then)

I'm serious. You should go.

JOHN *makes* CHARLIE *look at him;* CHARLIE *takes in his seriousness. Beat. Then—)*

JOHN: C'mon. We can listen to Sade on the way down.

(—as lights shift—)

(—and CHARLIE *and* JOHN *walk across stage to where* CASEY SIMMONS *stands waiting. He is a 19 year-old Black kid in a prison jumpsuit who can swing from hardened to vulnerable, closed-off to matter of fact, charming to utterly indifferent. His eyes are watchful; he takes in those before him.)*

CHARLIE: Hi—Casey? Charles Duff. And this is my colleague John Ebbs.

*(*CASEY *nods slightly…)*

CHARLIE: Should we sit?

(They sit.)

CHARLIE: So, ah, we came down here to visit some prisoners and, ah…

JOHN: After Charlie talked about the prison, we decided to meet some folks. And since you'd been in one of the reports, we thought we'd ask to see you.

(Beat)

CHARLIE: So where are you from, Casey?

CASEY: Rochester.

CHARLIE: Oh, okay. That's where we live. Just up the highway.

*(*CASEY *nods)*

CHARLIE: I'm the news anchor for Channel 10, John does sports.

CASEY: Yeah, they told me.

CHARLIE: Of course.

JOHN: How long've you been in prison?

CASEY: I got *here* three months ago. Before that I was in jail for a year, waiting for my trial.

JOHN: How old are you?

CASEY: Nineteen.

CHARLIE: And how's it going for you so far?

CASEY: It's fine. People try to mess with you but I just ignore 'em.

JOHN: How?

CASEY: Stay to myself.

CHARLIE: …May I ask what you're in for?

CASEY: No.

(Beat)

CHARLIE: How long is your sentence?

CASEY: Seventy-five years, but I'll probably do fifty.

JOHN: …Is there a way to lower that?

CASEY: They said you can get time cuts but probably only about three years worth.

CHARLIE: Time cuts for—?

CASEY: G E D. I think you get six months for that. You can do like a mentor program I guess, but I don't really know about that.

(CHARLIE and JOHN absorb all this…)

CHARLIE: Do you want us to buy you some chips or something? Fritos?

CASEY: No I don't want any Fritos.

CHARLIE: Okay.
(Pause)
What was it like to grow up in Rochester?

CASEY: Depends where you live. Parts of it aren't so nice.

JOHN: And which part were *you* in?

CASEY: *(A small smile)* The not so nice.

CHARLIE: Where's that?

CASEY: Plymouth Avenue.

(CHARLIE nods.)

CHARLIE: Do you have siblings, Casey?

CASEY: Two older sisters.

CHARLIE: And what do they think of you being in here?

CASEY: They were like, "Why'd you do that?" But they don't really understand the way I was living.

CHARLIE: And which way was that?

CASEY: You know, tryin' to be whatever. Runnin' around the wrong way. Wrong people, wrong situations.

JOHN: ...So you didn't finish high school?

(CASEY shakes his head.)

JOHN: Were you a good student?

CASEY: I mean, not really. But not bad. When I concentrated. I didn't really like school.

JOHN: Why not?

CASEY: I dunno. Did you?

JOHN: No.

CASEY: So then you know what I mean.

CHARLIE: *(Pause)* So what's this place like?

CASEY: Stupid. All you do is sit around tryin' not to get in fights. Someone told me they don't even hang Christmas lights at Christmas 'cause they don't wanna offend the people who don't celebrate Christmas, and

I was like, just 'cause they got some lights doesn't mean they out to *oppress* people. So he said that at the holidays we just gonna sit around with no lights and *make believe* we're celebratin'. An' I'm like, "What does that mean?" And he's like, "You can sing Christmas carols in your cell," an' I was like, "I ain't singin' no motherfuckin' *Jingle Bells* in my fuckin' cell." ...Sorry. I was tryin' not to curse.

CHARLIE: Why's that?

CASEY: 'Cause they told me you're religious.

CHARLIE: That's not really true.

CASEY: You're not religious?

CHARLIE: No.
(And then)
Well, I've been doing some religious, ah, *speaking*, but I'm not particularly religious myself.

(CASEY looks at CHARLIE... Then, to JOHN:)

CASEY: Are *you*?

JOHN: No. I probably should be, but no.

CASEY: Why *should* you be?

JOHN: It would probably help me get through the day better.

(CASEY just looks at JOHN.)

CHARLIE: So——have you *seen* our broadcast, Casey?

CASEY: Nope.

CHARLIE: Do you have access to T V?

CASEY: Yeah, we got T Vs in our cells so all we do is watch T V like fifteen hours a day.

CHARLIE: But you don't watch Channel 10 news?

JOHN: At six and eleven?

CASEY: *(A look)* I watch Discovery Channel.

JOHN: I watch that too. I like that.

CASEY: Right? You seen the one where they talk about birds in Canada?

JOHN: No.

CASEY: It's good. They got a bird there called a "red-necked grebe," and I was like *"whaat?"*—

JOHN: I fuckin' *hate* the redneck Grebe—

CHARLIE: The point is I recently started saying a prayer at the end of each broadcast, and some of them have actually sort of "come true".

(CASEY again just stares...)

CASEY: Serious?

CHARLIE: I mean it depends who you ask.

JOHN: It's a pretty amazing thing.

CASEY: ...That's cool.
(Pause)
But you gotta be careful what you pray for, right?

CHARLIE: That's right.

CASEY: *(Genuine)* Otherwise...
(Pause)
But it's cool.
(And then)
I'ma try an' watch you.
(And then)
Maybe.

(—as lights cross fade to the newsroom, where CHARLIES, JOHN, and SUE stand with ZOELLNER.)

ZOELLNER: It is my *responsibility* to properly navigate the relationship between the marketplace and God.

SUE: I thought you were "fighting the good fight" for journalistic neutrality.

ZOELLNER: That was *rhetoric,* Sue, this is reality.

SUE: And our sponsors?

ZOELLNER: Our sponsors are happy except for some of them. Some of them are "sad," which is sad, for *them.*

JOHN: Are they litigating?

ZOELLNER: Stick to stickball, John—

JOHN: *Oh C'MON!*—

CHARLIE: Can you just tell us what we're talking about exactly?

ZOELLNER: It's a global media start-up that wants to stream us live for the last five minutes at six and eleven; they also have a documentary crew that they *swear* will be unobtrusive—

CHARLIE: I don't know, Scott—

ZOELLNER: It's a *documentary!*

CHARLIE: It's reality T V.

ZOELLNER: *It's P B S!*

JOHN: No it's not—

ZOELLNER: Fine—*T B S.*

CHARLIE: It doesn't feel right.

ZOELLNER: Well that's what Moses said about killing, so you're on the right track.

JOHN: Should Roger be here for this?

ZOELLNER: Roger's in the weather-center looking for fog.

SUE: Scott, you stood here and said—

ZOELLNER: What I said was in reaction to the early *recklessness* of Charlie's prayers. What I am recognizing *now* is the larger context.

SUE: Which is what?

ZOELLNER: Which is that any geopolitical insight that your average American might glean from our program is immediately filtered through whatever theological *gauze* they've wrapped across their beady little eyes, so for us to hide behind false religious neutrality is nonsensical. If they can't leave God by the curb for half an hour, then we will embrace Him with *numinous fervor.*

SUE: Okay, besides being *offensive*, that triggers every journalistic red flag that exists on earth.

ZOELLNER: Well I'm sorry—

SUE: Well you should be—

ZOELLNER: Well I'm not because *Fox* shoves their shit down our throats twenty-four/seven and I don't see your Trail Of Tears for that.

SUE: I don't *work* for Fox—

ZOELLNER: So then what is it, Sue, because it's not like you don't like the ratings—

SUE: *I don't like that you're exploiting religion.*
(Pause)
As a person for whom religion is not a "joke", it's offensive to see it being used opportunistically, especially in regard to journalism, which itself should be sacred.
(And then, quieter)
Belief should be private; between one's self, one's God, and the person or notion for *whom one prays.*

(The others let this land....)

JOHN: You guys hear about that bar fight last night?

(They look up)

JOHN: Apparently some guy started saying that Charlie should have his tongue cut out for being un-American.
(More to CHARLIE*)*
But then like eight other guys defended you, saying *you* were the reason no one died when that prop plane went down in Churchville last week.

CHARLIE: What'd that have to do with me?

JOHN: You'd prayed for people's "safe travel" at the end of the show that night.

(CHARLIE *takes this in.*)

JOHN: Anyway—the tongue guy wasn't convinced and he kept calling for your public de-tongue-ing. So the eight guys beat the shit out of him—in the name of Charlie Duff. And now they refuse to plead guilty even though they're sober. They claim they were defending *God*. One of them used the word "crusade."

SUE: This is what I'm talking about, it's insane not to keep these things separate.

ZOELLNER: Look; Sue. You're right. When people react like that, it's insane. And as a person for whom religion *is* a joke, I respect that it's not one for you; I do. I'm actually a Catholic myself; with a slight case of alter-boy-P T S D.
(To CHARLIE*)*
Point is, the prayers are already on YouTube. Why not make it official?

CHARLIE: Because I don't want to inspire a crusade, Scott.

ZOELLNER: So then tell 'em how to act—

CHARLIE: I have no idea—

ZOELLNER: You've been telling them since day one!—

CHARLIE: Well now they're not *listening!*—

ZOELLNER: *Make* 'em listen!

CHARLIE: How?!—

ZOELLNER: Say it better!

CHARLIE: You know what—I'm done—no more prayers—

JOHN: Charlie—

CHARLIE: A *reality* show?!

ZOELLNER: It doesn't diminish your *power!*—

CHARLIE: Of course it does! It's what America does best: Turns genuine impulse into bullshit, low-brow entertainment. The moment you put yourself out there they will bludgeon you like a piece of fucking veal. So *no*—I will not be participating in the ritualistic neutering of the first honest thing I've done in years.

JOHN: Dude—

CHARLIE: *No.*
(Slightly calmer)
The people I'm praying for are real; they have lives, they have families, they have feelings, and you can't just package that for consumption.

(Silence; this is not the normal CHARLIE. ZOELLNER *absorbs; but a fighter himself, he takes a new tact.)*

TED: *(O S) Stand by for places!*

ZOELLNER: I understand all that. I do. You're a man of integrity. And I mean that.
(And then, honest)
But Charlie. I challenge you: Beat them at their own game. Transcend the bullshit and make us believe in something. Beneath the cynicism, and fear-mongering, and greed…make us understand each other in a way we forgot we could.

(Focused)
You have a power. It is effective, it is far-reaching, and it is yours.
(Near whisper)
Use it.

(CHARLIE *takes this in, not convinced.*)

(Lights shift and the others fade away. The light on CHARLIE *is now intense. Silence. He remains still, in deep contemplation… And then, slowly, he walks to the anchor desk and takes a seat.* JOHN *and* SUE *are there. As* CHARLIE *sits they are live on air:)*

SUE: That does it for us at 6, we'll see you at 11. For Roger in the weather center, for John, and from *all* of us here at Channel 10 News——

(SUE *awkwardly looks at* CHARLIE, *unsure what he's going to do. Silence, as he sits, himself not sure…)*

(And then he speaks, quietly and without knowing where he's going, and as he does—)

(—lights find mostly just him; his voice perhaps slightly mic'd; intimate.)

(As he speaks, his voice slowly, gradually, builds with a new-found poise, gentle but with confidence.)

CHARLIE: Seven years ago, while walking with my nine year-old son along a cliff overlooking the Genesee River, he turned to me and said, "This is the way it should be."
(Pause)
Which is a nice sentiment, and would have made me happy enough on its own, if it weren't for the fact that they were the exact same words, spoken in the same way, that my father had said to me when I was nineteen. He and I sitting in the tiny sun room of his apartment in Springfield, Oregon, Christmas vacation of my sophomore year in college. The winter sun was

coming in through the double-paned windows, there
was a pause in the conversation, and then he turned,
out of nowhere, and said, "This is the way it should
be."

(Pause)

When my son said that to me, over fifteen years
later…I suddenly knew, if only for a moment, that
there was possibly something else in going on in the
world…that I truly wasn't aware of.

(Pause)

Which is not to say the world's not broken; and that
the list of its *brokennes*…isn't sometimes overwhelming.

(Pause)

But it does make me wonder what would happen if we
all turned to one another, at the exact same time, and
reached out.

(Slowly gaining force)

To our neighbor, to the person we *don't* know, to our
fathers, our children, the people who mop our floors,
the people who run our banks, the people we've locked
away and forgotten—*everyone*; all of us reaching out,
with eyes closed, and saying to each other, "This
brokenness—is *not* the way it should be."

(Pause)

Would we generate something better? A force that
might somehow shift the planet forward, maybe just an
inch—but to a better, less ruinous place; to where there
truly *was* something else going on; due to our collective
will?

(Pause)

I don't have a prayer tonight; it's really just a question:
Is there a way to harness that power? To use it to
literally move the earth; and in so doing, somehow
shorten the length…of the list of the broken world?

(Pause)

It would certainly be nice.

(Pause)
Good night.

(Beat. Then lights go black.)

END OF ACT ONE

ACT TWO

(Video projection——as we hear:)

C N N REPORTER: *(V O)* And so it is that in this once-vibrant, now-struggling city, one man is making a multitude of difference.

(Video footage of a group of high school kids picking up roadside garbage.)

C N N REPORTER: *(V O)* Since going "on-air-with-prayer" one month ago, Rochester anchorman Charles Duff has lit a fire under this community;

(Video of a blind person being helped across an intersection by a red-haired Puerto Rican girl—)

C N N REPORTER: *(V O)* —inspiring acts of goodwill and, depending on whom you ask—divine intervention, through both television *and* prayer.

(Video of ZOELLNER in extreme close-up.)

ZOELLNER: *(Uncannily earnest)* What separates Charles is that he's not a televangelist; he's a serious news-journalist with twenty years experience who *happens* to have a cultivated spiritual side, which is the exact duality you want in someone making this type of crossover. The duality at play here is *breathtaking.*

(Video of the C N N REPORTER approaching CHARLIE as he makes his way through a crowd of supporters outside the station—)

C N N REPORTER: Charles, do you consider yourself God's mouthpiece for the city of Rochester?

CHARLIE: God doesn't need a mouthpiece.

C N N REPORTER: So then how do you explain this phenomenon?

CHARLIE: I don't.

(Video of Rochester school kids—Arab, Asian, Latinx, African—all getting along—)

C N N REPORTER: *(V O)* Always humble, *possibly* deific, Charles Duff claims that all he's doing is performing his job and speaking his heart.

(Video of a rock concert, the band playing beneath a "BENEFIT FOR CHARLES DUFF PRAYER RECIPIENTS" banner.)

C N N REPORTER: *(V O)* But these days in Rochester, there are a lot of people who think he's doing a whole lot more.

(Video of the supporters outside the station, holding signs and candles—)

C N N REPORTER: *(V O)* For C N N Prime Time, this is Cindy Rodriguez in Rochester, New York.

(The projection ends as lights shift—)

(CHARLIE and RICK outside RICK's school, mid-argument.)

CHARLIE: I understand why you think I'm a hypocrite—

RICK: Do you?—

CHARLIE: I do and you have to listen—

RICK: Why?—

CHARLIE: *(Strong)* Because I'm your Dad and I'm *saying* so.

RICK: Roger that, Pops.

CHARLIE: ...I want us to communicate in a meaningful way. Or at least try.

RICK: This isn't that kind of movie.

CHARLIE: I don't even know what that—

RICK: You don't get to act like an asshole for sixteen years and then walk back in, hand me a Coke and rub my hair. It doesn't work like that. People make their decisions and they have to *live* with them.

CHARLIE: Is that right?—

RICK: It's totally right—

CHARLIE: And are you making the right decisions?—

RICK: Totally—

CHARLIE: You sure?—

RICK: Totally—

CHARLIE: Why?—

RICK: Because *I* don't need the kind of "guidance" you seem to wanna offer me when you're not busy offering it to the *rest* of Rochester, because I can actually figure things out on my own. We may have had a "good moment" on some cliff when I was nine but that is not some kind of get-outta-jail-free card seven years later. I have my friends, my mother, my brain and a knowledge of what total bullshit is—*so please just stop trying to pretend you know me!* Because you don't. You don't know me. You have *no* idea.
(And then)
And so if praying on T V is what gets you going right now, then go for it, but don't think it's gonna have an effect on me, 'cause it's not. I'm beyond your reach.
(He turns and starts to go—)

CHARLIE: *Rick.*

(RICK pauses, not turning back.)

CHARLIE: That's all good and fine and I respect it. But I wanna say one last thing. I turned away from my dad at a certain point and it screwed me up. Right up to now and who knows for how much more.

(Strong)

So let me just say before you walk away like the rebellious little dude that I know you would like to be right now: I wanna know you again. I desperately wanna know you. And so I will keep coming after you until the day that I stop at which point it'll be too late. So *until* that day, keep an open mind, because I happen to know that after it passes, *I* will grow old and die alone, and *you*—if you're not careful—will turn into a miserable little fuck.

(Pause)

So stay open to it, Rick; that's all I'm saying. Stay open.

(Pause. JOHN enters.)

JOHN: Charlie—we should probably go if we wanna get there.

CHARLIE: Right. John, this is my son, Rick.

JOHN: Oh—hey, bud, how're you doin'?

RICK: Good.

JOHN: Nice shirt.

(To CHARLIE)

Why can't we be that hip?

CHARLIE: No idea.

RICK: …I liked your story about high school wrestling.

JOHN: *(Genuine)* Ah—thanks, bud. That was a while ago—

RICK: Yeah—

JOHN: But hey—that means a lot.

RICK: You're the only part of that show that speaks truth.

JOHN: *(Genuine) Thanks*, Rick.
(And then)
But hey—pretty cool what your *Dad's* up to these days too, no?

RICK: …I guess.

JOHN: He's a good man.
(Pause—then:)
So did I once hear you play basketball?

RICK: I used to but now I'm in a band.

JOHN: You know what?—I'm fine with that. I wish *I'd* played in a band in high school instead of, like, playing fuckin' baseball. I mean really, who needs that much baseball?

(Off CHARLIE's *look)*

JOHN: Sorry—I shouldn't cuss so much, although if you're in a band you probably do some serious cussing. I mean that was the problem with *baseball*, all the curse words were like—
(Southern accent)
"Aww shucks, Jimmy-Joe, I'm hittin' one-ninety-eight goddammit!"
(Then, to RICK)
I imagine you guys have better cuss words than that.

RICK: We do.

JOHN: Like what?

RICK: Like *Fuck-it-to-the max.*

JOHN: "Fuck-it to the max?"

RICK: Yeah, Fuck-it-to-the-max, and, ah, "Fuck dunce".

JOHN: Wait—you say Fuck-dunce? I say Fuck-dunce too!

RICK: Seriously?

JOHN: I'm totally serious! Charlie—do I not say Fuck-dunce?

CHARLIE: You do, you say fuck-dunce—

JOHN: I do!—
(To RICK*)*
C'mere, I'm gonna give you a hug.
(He hugs RICK…*)*

CHARLIE: We should go.

JOHN: Right.
(To RICK*)*
Good to finally meet you, bud.

RICK: You too.

CHARLIE: Rick.

*(*RICK *pauses,)*

CHARLIE: Bye.

(Lights shift—)

(And we are in the prison visitors room where CHARLIE *and* JOHN *wait as* CASEY *enters in his prison jumpsuit.)*

CHARLIE: So can you tell us what happened?

CASEY: They put me in segregated.

JOHN: Why?

CASEY: They said to protect me from gangs but reality is they just don't like me.

CHARLIE: Why don't they like you?

CASEY: 'Cause I ain't playing their game.

CHARLIE: Which game?

CASEY: Of believin' what they say, that they keep their word, 'cause they don't. Like all that stuff they supposed to be doin' with the money that came in because of your prayers. Talkin' about how it's being used for "programs"—but it's bullshit. They ain't got no programs, all they got is D O L jobs pay you twenty-five cents a day to make some fuckin' *signs* so they can sell that shit and keep the money for themselves. I saw the warden on T V talkin' about how great it is for what you did but it's not *real*, man, 'cause there ain't been no difference in here since that happened. And it's not just me sayin' that, it's everyone in here saying it's been like that since whenever they came in.

CHARLIE: Maybe it takes time to reach you guys.

CASEY: It's a *lie*. Even if they're nice people it's a lie 'cause of the way the system works. I mean even if they *did* give us a book—*then* what? I read a book behind some bars for the rest of my life? I'm supposed to be *thankful* for that?

JOHN: ...I hear what you're saying, Casey, but why exactly did they put you in segregated housing?

CASEY: ...'Cause I spat on a guard.

CHARLIE: Why?

CASEY: 'Cause he ripped down the sheet I had over my bars an' called me a fuckin' orphan.

JOHN: An *orphan?*

(CASEY *nods.*)

JOHN: Why'd he call you that?

CASEY: 'Cause my Mom ain't come to visit me yet.
(Pause)
It's 'cause she been staying with my sister downstate.

JOHN: *(Pause)* It's against the rules to have a sheet up over your bars?

(CASEY *nods.*)

JOHN: So why'd you do it?

CASEY: Someone lent me a phone so I was trying to make a call.

JOHN: To your Mom?

(CASEY *doesn't say no.*)

CHARLIE: And so how long were you segregated?

CASEY: Two weeks. Got out yesterday.

JOHN: *(Pause)* What's it like in there?

CASEY: Bad.

JOHN: Why?

CASEY: 'Cause you're sitting in a cell you can barely lie down in, twenty-three hours a day, you can't talk to no one, you start thinking dark thoughts, like you just wanna....
(Pause)
You get so fucking alone. It's like you get really sad. And then you get…mad; like you wanna fuckin' kill people. And then you just realize you're still alone. Like totally alone.

(JOHN *takes this in; maybe a nod…*)

CASEY: I even tried to pray.
(And then)
I was like, might as well give it a try.

CHARLIE: Did it help?

CASEY: *No.* I mean, maybe if I'd kept *t*ryin', but I was like, it ain't fair for me to all of a sudden start prayin' just cause I'm in here. Didn't seem like good deal for God.

CHARLIE: I'm sure he wouldn't have minded.

CASEY: Not for me to say.
(And then)
Maybe for *you,* but not me.

(Beat)

CASEY: I ain't saying I don't deserve to be here. 'Cause I do. But you don't gotta treat us without graciousness.

(Beat)

CHARLIE: Why do you say you deserve to be here?

CASEY: Yo you're not supposed to *ask* me that!

CHARLIE: Why—

CASEY: *'Cause it's supposed to be private!*

CHARLIE: ...I'm sorry.

CASEY: *(Long pause)* I'm in here 'cause...I shot a kid; point blank in his chest. And didn't do nothin' to help him. Just stood there and watched. Stood there and jus'...

CHARLIE: ...Why did you shoot him?

CASEY: My friend and me was supposed to rob him, and we didn't realize he was gonna have his man with him too but we went ahead anyway, so when we pulled *our* gun he pulled his, and he shot at my friend, so *I* shot him.

(Pause)

And he bled out right there.

CHARLIE: Was he someone you knew?

CASEY: ...A little.

CHARLIE: And why didn't you do anything to help him?

CASEY: ...I don't know. Wish I had.

JOHN: Like what?

CASEY: I dunno.

(Pause)

Talked to him as he died.

(Pause)

Somethin' with graciousness.

(*Beat…*)

So the armed robbery plus the murder, that's why I'm in for so long.

(*Pause*)

But like I say, I just wanna do my time in dignity an' get out.

(CHARLIE *and* JOHN *absorb this…*)

(*Silence*)

(*Loud sound of a prison buzzer*)

CASEY: That's me.

(*And* CASEY *heads back inside the prison.* CHARLIE *and* JOHN *stand alone. Both are in their own head, but perhaps for different reasons. Beat…*)

JOHN: My Dad died when I was ten and my Mom was pretty checked out after that. I didn't have siblings so I used to, like, call *myself* an "orphan". I actually took pride in it. Then one day I realized that being lonely really wasn't fun.

(*Pause*)

I was probably about the same age as him. And I was like, "Shit, this isn't good." But I didn't know what to do about it.

(*Then, lighter*)

I like that he tried to pray.

(CHARLIE *absorbs.*)

CHARLIE: Wanna know the last time I prayed before all this? Ten years ago.

(*Pause*)

C B S brought me in for a network position. Thinking about grooming me for "the chair". And the night before the interview I was at the hotel bar, midtown Manhattan, gorgeous spring night. And I'm talking to

this woman who asks why I'm in town, and I turn and
say, "I'm here to be the next Dan Rather. Only better."
Which of course she loved, that I was cocky, good
enough looking. Putty in my hands.
(Pause)
So after she left, as I was falling asleep, I prayed.

JOHN: For forgiveness?

CHARLIE: To get the job the next day. First time I'd
prayed since I was a kid and I ask to become a rich,
famous anchorman who could get laid whenever he
wants. Which I considered a legitimate fringe benefit.
This, twenty minutes after being unfaithful to my wife.

JOHN: And do you think that's what you're doing now?
Praying for the wrong reasons?

CHARLIE: ...Do *you?*

JOHN: Doesn't matter what I think. What matters is if it
helps.

(CHARLIE and JOHN again stand for a moment...)

(—as we hear a voicemail message:)

LISA: *(O S)* Charlie, it's Lisa. So—because this is how
things seem to work these days—Rick has indicated
that he might be willing to tolerate your presence at
his "rock concert" Thursday night, at Delano's at ten,
which, given his previous *in*tolerance, is equivalent to
the opening of China. I'm in Boston for a conference
that night so I'd actually appreciate it too. Anyway,
after picking my jaw up from the floor, I told him I'd
ask you. So...here I am. Let me know?

(CHARLIE is already dialing—)

CHARLIE: Lisa, it's Charlie. Tell Rick I'll be there and
that I'm psyched. Well, don't say that, just say I'm
happy to have been invited and I'll see him there.
Thank you. Bye.

(Lights shift. CHARLIE, *now in his office, lost in thought. After a moment* SUE *is there. He looks up.)*

CHARLIE: Hey.

SUE: Hi.

CHARLIE: You okay?

SUE: Yeah.

CHARLIE: ...Can I get you something? You want a Snapple?

SUE: No thanks.

CHARLIE: *(Pause)* Sue?

SUE: I wanna leave my husband.

CHARLIE: *(Pause as he takes this in)* Really?

SUE: It's not working. Hasn't been for a long time. And, um, I'm wondering if you think I should.

CHARLIE: ...Why isn't it working?

SUE: We have different ways of dealing with our son. We didn't at first. Then we did. So that's how it started.

CHARLIE: And now?

SUE: And now we barely communicate, we sleep in separate rooms, we haven't *touched* each other in.... what feels like years.
(She is standing very still, eyes perhaps closed)
You try so hard to make things work. You do a million things you don't want to. You smile when you wanna cry; you tidy up when you want to...wreak havoc. I make eighty per cent of the money, I do ninety per cent of the work around the house, I care for our child, I try to be a loving person and then my husband tells me I have a pole up my ass. It's not...how I was meant to live.
(Maybe opening her eyes)

I used to be a loving person, Charles. I used to be fucking care-free, I swear to God. I used to have... wanderlust; I used to collect bugs; I used to make sweet potato pancakes; I used to want to take flying lessons; I used to listen to a hundred different types of music; I used to fix everything that was broken in the house; I used to cut my own hair; I used to take my son to the park every Saturday to play with his boat in the pond. And now I look at myself...and I'm a stranger. I'm a shell. I don't like drinking my coffee in the morning anymore, I don't hum in the shower, I don't buy interesting underwear, I don't bake people birthday cakes, I don't dance, I don't enjoy my job, I don't like my husband, I don't kiss my son enough, I don't...

(Near whisper)

...I don't know what I'm doing.

(At a total loss, CHARLIE *steps to* SUE *and gives her a hug, part reassurance, part healing. They stand like this a moment....and then she kisses him on the lips. It is less a kiss of fiery passion than of quiet, gentle longing.)*

(The kiss lasts for several moments ...before CHARLIE *pulls away, less from "propriety" —for lust is not foreign to him—than from slight confusion, at least for the moment.* SUE *regards him—)*

(...and then she takes a step back.)

SUE: I'm sorry.

CHARLIE: It's okay.

SUE: *(Pause)* I'll see you at eleven.

*(*SUE *turns and leaves;* CHARLIE *watches.)*

*(*CHARLIE *now making his way along a quiet street. An* UNSHAVEN MAN *with a black beanie walks by, does a double-take:)*

UNSHAVEN MAN: Hey—you're Duff, right?

CHARLIE: …Yeah.

UNSHAVEN MAN: *(Gentle)* I saw your little prayer last week, about moving the earth? Well you know what I would like?
(Strong)
I'd like you to fuck off! You want us to move the earth?—It's already moving: *GLOBAL FUCKING WARMING! I'd like to see your "magical earth-moving prayers" move THAT one back to how it was!*

CHARLIE: If you don't like it don't listen—

(CHARLIE *moves on but the* UNSHAVEN MAN *follows—)*

UNSHAVEN MAN: Well I *did* listen, dude! It's the *NEWS!* And you know what I didn't like?! —What I *don't* like?!

(CHARLIE *hesitates.)*

UNSHAVEN MAN: "He who offers false consolation"!

(CHARLIE *pushes past the* UNSHAVEN MAN)

UNSHAVEN MAN: Religion kills, fucker! It's a man-made weapon that kills those who need it most! *You're killing the innocent, Duff!*

(CHARLIE *is gone, the stage empty but for the* UNSHAVEN MAN. *Who then throws in—)*

UNSHAVEN MAN: *And what the fuck does your sports guy have against the Bills!?*

(—as light shift…)

(And the video shows a crowd of college kids holding "DOWN WITH DUFF" signs during a loud and vehement protest—)

RON: *(O S)* —and many of these young folks are *determined* to make clear their opinion that Charles Duff is *not* the next Messiah.

(Close-up on an indignant 20-SOMETHING PROTESTER *being interviewed by* RON.*)*

20-SOMETHING PROTESTER: My grandparents came to this country to get *away* from opiate-dispensers like Duff, so when I turn on the news I want *truth,* not some candy-assed faker singing cum-by-ya!

*(*RON *reports from a leafy college campus—)*

RON: And it's not just students. I also spoke with a media studies professor who finds the phenomenon alarming.

(Close -up on a grizzled but DISTINGUISHED PROFESSOR.*)*

DISTINGUISHED PROFESSOR: The problem with Duff is that he clearly hasn't read his own Bible, otherwise he'd have gotten to Matthew 6:5, which states: "When you pray, do not be like the hypocrites who love to pray publicly on the street corners to be seen by men. For I guarantee this truth: *That will be their only reward."*
(Soberly, directly to camera)
Charles Duff is a classic false prophet.

(Footage of the college protesters sticking up the middle finger and shouting: IM-POS-TER! IM-POS-TER!*)*

(Camera pulls back to reveal RON *in the foreground, shouting above the din:)*

RON: And so you can see, while Charles Duff has clearly lit a fire in this community, we must also note that fire sometimes *burns.* From the U-Rock campus in south Rochester, this is Ron Kirkpatrick!

(—as the video fades and the anchors, now seated, absorb a moment.)

SUE: ...Well. Thank you, Ron.
(To CHARLIE, *attempted perkiness)*
I guess it just goes to show, everyone's got an opinion.

JOHN: Even Gandhi had his bad days.

SUE: That does it for us at six, we'll see you at eleven. And now, *Charles.*

(CHARLIE *takes a moment… And then:*)

CHARLIE: If there weren't people shouting, we'd be in deep trouble. So tonight…I'll let those shouting have the last word.

(Pause)

Have a good night.

(Music swells and they are now off-air.)

TED: *(O S) Clear!*

JOHN: Well *that* was interesting.

SUE: But it's good we ran it.

CHARLIE: Absolutely.

(Silence as they take off their mics.)

(More silence, JOHN *and* SUE *both looking at* CHARLIE *but trying not to stare.* ZOELLNER *enters. He says nothing for a moment…and then:)*

ZOELLNER: I need to tell you guys something.

(They note his tone)

ZOELLNER: There's been an incident down at Five Points Prison with that kid you've gotten to know.
(To CHARLIE *and* JOHN*)*
The kid you guys have visited. Casey Simmons?

CHARLIE: What happened?

ZOELLNER: Apparently he refused to leave his cell after they found a smuggled phone in there, so they… extracted him. He fought back and was, it seems, severely beaten. Ruptured spleen, massive internal bleeding, left unconscious in his cell for five hours before they decided he needed help. He was sent to Providence, but…he's now on life support. I'm sorry.

(Silence)

JOHN: …Jesus.

SUE: He's not gonna make it?

ZOELLNER: They don't think so. The bleeding was…a major hemorrhage.

CHARLIE: Did they…how'd you find out?

ZOELLNER: An inmate from Five Points called the station. Wanted us to run a story. I just followed up at the hospital.

SUE: *Should* we run a story?

ZOELLNER: …My instinct is that it's not newsworthy.

CHARLIE: What are you talking about?—

ZOELLNER. We still don't know the details—

CHARLIE: *They beat a man to death, Scott—*

ZOELLNER: They extracted an inmate from his cell, it happens everyday—

CHARLIE: Yeah—and we've been running stories about prison reform at *that* fucking prison—

ZOELLNER: I'm not saying we don't report it, we just need facts—

CHARLIE: I think you just wanna *duck* the fact that we raised fifty grand for a place that kills people—

SUE: It's more than just that—

CHARLIE: *How?—*

SUE: We can't jump to conclusions based on a phone call—

CHARLIE: Well actually we *can—*

SUE: We need to send someone out to understand the context—

CHARLIE: The context is that our Five Points coverage generated half a million hits and now we look like assholes.

ZOELLNER: *(Calm but forceful) Exactly*—and if you watched Ron's report you'll note that people are calling you a fraud, so it is *not* in our interest to jump on a story we know *very* little about. What if this guy injured officers on his way to getting beat? What if he's in for murder and has been attacking officers since he got there? What if they were just following policy? It is our job to *not* let liberal predilections dictate our taking sides, and I'm sorry but that is the reaction you're having. You're taking it personally because you knew the kid, and *that* does not constitute journalism.
(And then)
So we'll find out more and evaluate *tomorrow*.

(ZOELLNER leaves; CHARLIE watches, not quite believing; he turns to SUE—)

CHARLIE: You don't think he's being completely hypocritical?

SUE: I think he's right to be worried.

CHARLIE: We're talking about someone *being beaten within an inch of their life!*

SUE: Someone you *also* happen to have befriended, which from where *I* sit means you'll end up also *praying* for him. And you can't pray on T V *just* for your favorite friends, Charlie. It's like if I were to ask you to pray for my son. Whatever you're doing—*can't* work that way. It defies the whole idea.
(And then)
Which is maybe why you should take a beat.

(SUE exits. CHARLIE is now alone with JOHN, who is quietly devastated…)

(After a moment he speaks, almost to himself.)

JOHN: I'm an asshole. Sitting here thinking things make sense: You pray for things to get better. People get excited, things get better. But they don't. ...Things don't get better. Throw around all the money you want, pray and be happy, but in the end, a kid like that...dies a nameless death. Fucking dies alone. ... And no one gives a shit. Light all the candles you want, he's still alone.

CHARLIE: John—

JOHN: *Stop.*
(Quieter)
There's nothing good you can spin that into. The planet moved forward...then it moved right back again; to where it most likely belongs.
(Pause; almost internal)
I mean, can you imagine getting beaten to *death?* There've gotta be better ways to go.
(And then, looking up; simple, almost casual)
If I had to go, I'd want it to be water. Fall into some water, crystal blue, lose myself in the depth. Float back up to the top. Then just sorta bob around the seas of the world, taking in the sun, the moon...maybe a bird lands on me to take a rest.

CHARLIE: That's actually not how it works; when you fall into water, you drown, and then you're dead. It's not poetic.

JOHN: It's my soul that would be floating.
(And then)
I'm just saying, no one should die by getting beaten. It lacks graciousness.
(He stands to go.)

(—as lights shift and we hear:)

LOCAL REPORTER: *(V O)* A breaking story out of Providence Hospital this morning where a nineteen year-old inmate named Casey Simmons has been placed on life support following an incident involving correctional officers at Five Points Prison. We go live now to the hospital and our reporter Al Bevins.

(—CHARLIE *stands alone on an empty stage; he doesn't move; his eyes remain closed.)*

LOCAL REPORTER #2: *(V O)* Thanks, Dana, crowds here have begun gathering in the hope that Channel 10 anchor Charles Duff might take up the case of Simmons, who was beaten at the same prison that Duff cited in his prayers last month, leading to over fifty thousand dollars in donations earmarked for *reform.*

(CHARLIE *continues to stand, motionless, as the audio plays on:)*

LOCAL REPORTER #2: *(V O)* As you know, for the last six weeks Duff has been inspiring acts of good will, communal harmony and, some say, performing downright otherworldly feats—but *no one* knows what his next prayer will be when it comes to the case of this convicted *killer,* whose mother is now faced with the decision of whether or not to take him off life support—

(Silence. CHARLIE *slowly opens his eyes.* ZOELLNER *is there.)*

CHARLIE: I guess the story got out anyway.

ZOELLNER: At first I thought you leaked it. Which would've made *this* a fun talk. But it turns out the inmate who called us then called Channel 4. Guess he didn't trust me.

CHARLIE: It's not a big leap, Scott.

ZOELLNER: …Did you go to the hospital?

CHARLIE: They wouldn't let me in. Wouldn't even let me on the same floor. "Security concerns."

(ZOELLNER *nods; beat.*)

ZOELLNER: You can't pray for his recovery, Charlie.

CHARLIE: Why not?

ZOELLNER: Because he's not *gonna* recover.

(Pause)

It's not even a close call. He's not a rundown soup kitchen in need of some spoon donations; he's a corpse pumping air by machine. It's not gonna happen.

CHARLIE: Sometimes it happens.

ZOELLNER: It never fucking happens. It happens once every hundred years.

(Then)

The kid's abdominal aorta was torn open. His organs are dysfunctional. The doctors have given up. Let the man die.

(Calmer)

Pray for him to find peace on his way *to* death. Be creative. But don't pray for him to recover.

(And then)

If you pray for the *impossible*, Charlie, you lose everything. Forget about me, or Sue, or John—if you pray for this, he will still die, and this will be over. You need to realize that.

(CHARLIE *doesn't answer;* ZOELLNER *turns to leave, then turns back.*)

ZOELLNER: And one more thing, C N N is simulcasting tonight's broadcast.

CHARLIE: You're unbelievable.

ZOELLNER: It's not my call. They set it up through New York after the story got picked up. So just remember: Whatever you say—it's going national.

(ZOELLNER *leaves.* CHARLIE *stands. The stage is again empty. Desolate. After a moment, he gives a short whistle, as if putting out a feeler to see if anyone's there. But no one is.*)

(CHARLIE *closes his eyes. After a beat, quiet, to himself, barely audible:*)

CHARLIE: *For we walk by faith, not by sight.*
(*Silence. He opens his eyes.*)

(*And then…*CHARLIE *steps to the news desk, where* SUE *is just taking her place.*)

(*As he sits, he notices* JOHN's *absence.*)

CHARLIE: Where's John?

SUE: He called in sick.

(*Beat, as* CHARLIE *glances at* JOHN's *empty chair…and then the pre-show music starts—as lights shift and suddenly they're on air.*)

SUE: That's it for Channel 10 at Six. The top story we'll be following in the newsroom: Casey Simmons clings to life at Rochester's Providence Hospital. And now, Charles.

(*As* CHARLIE *readies to speak, the video projects his image, along with the caption, "Rochester Anchorman Charles Duff speaks live about Casey Simmons". It's indeed going national.*)

(*Silence. It seems* CHARLIE *has no idea how or why he's going to do this. And then, as though recklessly leaving it to fate:*)

CHARLIE: Before we sign off tonight, I'd like to say a prayer for Casey Simmons, the inmate at the Five Points Correctional Facility in Romulus, New York, whose condition is indeed quite severe.

(*Video shows an enlarged mug shot of* CASEY.)

CHARLIE: I ask everyone watching, across the country, those who are inclined, to take a moment, as connected individuals, digitally and otherwise, knowing that the power of prayer *can* and often *does* affect, physically, the energy of the body, even for those we don't know: I ask that we pray.

(Bowing his head; simple but increasingly stronger)

I ask that Casey may emerge from his coma. I ask God to guide him back.

(And then)

And I pray that he may not only regain consciousness and recover the ability to breathe on his own, but that once he does, I pray he may return to prison with... support; from prison officials, from the community at large; the same community he so harmed when he committed his crime. I pray that he may be provided with opportunities for rehabilitation and eventual *reassimilation* into society, with the fullness of his life still before him, not behind. And that if so provided, that we the community will have *faith*—in Casey, and in ourselves—to sit with him, to wait for him, to not forget, to not abandon, to help him *live*, in our world, with our love.

(And then)

I pray for this.

(Stillness. CHARLIE remains with his head lowered. Sue the same. And then—)

CHARLIE: Good night.

(Lights shift suddenly as music begins and the video, starting slowly—shows a gradually momentous whirlwind of images: Some we have seen— [CHARLIE's life, his prayers, CASEY, his Dad, EMILY...], others brand new:)

(CHARLIE's supporters, kids with distended bellies, 30-car pile-ups, people winning Super Bowls, frogs having sex, NASCAR, Google Earth space shots, celebrity chefs, wars,

*famine, terrorism, crowds with "FUCK CHARLIE DUFF"
signs—the world.)*

*(As the images increase in speed, the music—perhaps
a theme that's been developing in fragments throughout
the play—begins to reach a climax, but it isn't a climax of
enlightenment—it's one bordering on chaos—chaos and
distortion and all kinds of fucked up flux—until suddenly:)*

*(Sound of a brick hurled at the video, exploding the screen
and shattering all sound and image entirely—but for:)*

(CHARLIE alone on stage in single shaft of light:)

(Silence)

(He is alone, in his head, eyes closed.)

*(…And then, finally, Zoellner is there…and we are back in
the studio.)*

(—as chants of "DUFF" slowly build in the distance…)

ZOELLNER: I had to hire a security firm for crowd
control. It's costing me ten grand a week.

CHARLIE: You can put an end to it any time.

ZOELLNER: By firing you? Because I take it that's what
you want. By praying for the kid and openly defying
me.

CHARLIE: I guess.

ZOELLNER: Not to mention casually calling for a radical
restructuring of the country's entire correctional
system.

CHARLIE: I thought I'd give it a try.

ZOELLNER: Right.
(Beat)
You know, Charlie, I fuck whores. Did you know that?

CHARLIE: …I did not.

ZOELLNER: I do and I'm pretty good at it, even though it gives me "guilt" due to the existence of my wife.
(Pause)
As you know, Charlie, things don't always work out the way you want in life. You graduate with honors, you meet your wife at sports bar, she's hot, *sexy... sporty.* You marry her and eight years later she's wearing ill-fitting jeans and insisting you buy a house on a lake.
(Pause)
Next thing you know you're boning a girl named Oblinka in a Days Inn off 490.

CHARLIE: ...Is there something you want me to say, Scott?

ZOELLNER: Well...*absolution* would be nice, but...I just thought you should know. Given the circumstances.

CHARLIE: Which circumstances?

ZOELLNER: ...I got a call from the hospital a couple minutes ago.

(CHARLIE looks at ZOELLNER.)

ZOELLNER: Casey awoke from his coma.
(Pause)
Not only that, they scanned him, and the aortic tear that caused the bleeding seems to have... "magically coalesced"; to the point where they think they can surgically repair it. Fully.

(CHARLIE looks atZOELLNER.)

ZOELLNER: As for the organ damage caused by the bleeding?—No longer an issue.

CHARLIE: ...Is that—?

ZOELLNER: Highly fucking unusual. The doctor I spoke to said it's not *unheard* of, but that it's highly, *highly...* highly unusual.

(Beat…quiet)
I have the impulse to hug you.

CHARLIE: …Okay.

(ZOELLNER steps to CHARLIE and hugs him.)

CHARLIE: You're not very consistent, Scott.

ZOELLNER: What can I say? I love my wife but I fuck whores.
(As he goes)
You did it, Charlie.

(—as we hear the opening notes of something like Buffalo Springfield's Something's Happening Here—*)*

C N N ANCHOR: *(O S)* They're calling it *The Miracle In Rochester.* Charles Duff's successful national prayer for prison inmate Casey Simmons heard here on C N N, has *transfixed* the country and overnight turned the issue of prayer into water cooler debate from Connecticut to California.

(As the song's lyrics now kick in and we watch CHARLIE step into his apartment, a small smile on his face. He stands, lost in thought, then slowly and deliberately begins to put on a tie and jacket—higher end clothes than we've seen him wear up to now.)

(We continue listening to the song as the video plays images of Japanese T V crews setting up outside the Channel 10 offices, and CHARLIE sitting on a T V studio couch with Savannah Guthrie, and Tibetan monks—in Tibet—smiling as they watch CHARLIE on their tiny Tibetan TV's, and cable news pundits arguing over CHARLIE, his head-shot looming above them, and Joe Rogan and Morning Joe and Rachel Maddow and Hannity and Friends—all of them talking CHARLIE…)

(—as CHARLIE now puts on his coat and we hear the sound of an airplane—)

(And now CHARLIE *steps into the aura of a New York office suite oozing L E D projections of warm blue light splashed upon a wall-embedded waterfall.)*

*(*CHARLIE *takes it in….)*

(And is then approached by TIM BREWER, *khakis and a sleeveless Patagonia; the confidence of a man who runs one of the largest media-entertainment companies in the world.)*

BREWER: Charles—Tim Brewer—welcome to New York, I'm so glad you could make it.

CHARLIE: Thanks for the jet.

BREWER: Isn't that nifty? Hawker 800XP; *solar panels on the wings.*

CHARLIE: Very cool.

BREWER: Smooth flight?

CHARLIE: Very.

BREWER: Excellent.
(Pause; a very small but genuine smile)
I'm glad we're meeting.

CHARLIE: Me too.

BREWER: What you did last night was…astonishing. I wanna say it had *canonical prowess* but I'm not sure that covers it.
(Cutting to chase)
There's an opportunity here, Charlie, as I'm sure you know, to take what you do and apply it to a *very* large canvass.
(A polite smile)
I know your history a little. I know there was once talk of the anchor job at C B S.

CHARLIE: That's true.

BREWER: Well if I'd been running N B C-Universal back *then,* I'd probably have come after you for our little flagship.
(And then)
But this is not then, and we're not your mother's N B C.
(Not even the smile)
There is more than just a vacancy at the top of the news division here, Charlie. There's a chance to entirely remake the way we deliver news and who we deliver it *to.* An opportunity to crack open what it means to *reach people.* I'm not talking about five nights a week at six-thirty, I'm talking deep, frictionless, *scalable* penetration into emerging markets *across the planet,* markets eager and open to your pantheistic, *pluralistic* approach to spirituality.

CHARLIE: Tim?—

BREWER: Charlie?—

CHARLIE: I didn't come down for a vocab quiz.

BREWER: *(A small smile)* Of course not.
(The smile disappears)
Put it this way: By 2050, *half* of all young people in the world will live in Africa. What if, *together,* we could reach those people.
(And then)
What if we reached those numbers across *six continents;* every single day?

CHARLIE: Through a news show?

BREWER: The term "news show" is antiquated.

CHARLIE: Why?

BREWER: Because right now there are dairy farmers in Kenya using I-Pads to track their cows; Malaysian migrants streaming TED talks on their factory floor;

rural Indonesians with no access to medical care being implanted with microchips to help them detect heart disease before it's too late—

CHARLIE: Meaning—?

BREWER: Technology has allowed us to reach people instantaneously, globally, anywhere, anytime. We need someone to reach them *with*.

CHARLIE: To advertise?

BREWER: *(Simple)* To be there for them.
(Then)
Look, I understand your cynicism; I used to have it too. But at a certain point it's too easy.

CHARLIE: ...So you provide access, but what about content?

BREWER: The content is up to you. News, prayer, *spiritual guidance in the wake of a tsunami.* It would be up to you. For us the content is *connection.* We're the medium, you're the message.
(And then)
People need the "brokeness of the world" explained to them in a humanistic way. That's what you do. And so we want *you* to explain the broken world to *fifty million people a night.* Remind us that we're in this together.

CHARLIE: ...And why would that many people listen to *me?*

BREWER: Because you transcend. You exceed the limitations of poverty, wealth, nationalism, race, class, partisanship, preference, denomination. You connect us, man! And in so doing, you generate compassion; and in so doing *that,* you turn the wheel of progress.
(Genuine)
All *we're* offering is a bigger wheel.
(Pause)

CHARLIE: What would be the next step?

BREWER: Move to New York, help us conceive a new *definition* of news; then be the face of it, the body of it, the "soul" of it.

CHARLIE: …I need time to think.

BREWER: Good—think. Imagine. *Imagine what you can do.* And then ask yourself: Don't I have an obligation?

CHARLIE: To do what?

BREWER: Make us live better.

(*—as lights shift…and* CHARLIE *stands, impressed.*)

(CHARLIE *now makes his way back into his apartment, the suit jacket and tie coming off.*)

(*He stands, taking it all in…*)

(*It is now the next morning. Beat…*)

CHARLIE: (*Calling off*) I made some coffee if you want.

(*No answer; then a moment later* SUE *emerges from the bedroom wearing an overlarge T-shirt of* CHARLIE's.)

SUE: I'm trying to quit.

CHARLIE: Why?

SUE: I don't know.

(CHARLIE *and* SUE *regard one another.*)

CHARLIE: It's okay I called last night?

SUE: Apparently.
(*A smile; then*)
Besides, isn't that what you do?

CHARLIE: No.
(*And then*)
Once upon a time, but…this was different.

SUE: We don't have to play that.

CHARLIE: Play what?

SUE: The expectation game.

CHARLIE: ...Okay.

SUE: I left James.

CHARLIE: (*Absorbing*) When?

SUE: Two days ago. Luke and I are staying with my sister.
(*And then*)
I didn't tell you last night because I didn't want this to have that layer. It's only important to *me*.

CHARLIE: Okay. But does it have to be only important to—?

SUE: Yes.

CHARLIE: Why?

SUE: Because we're co-workers; and because I don't want it.
(*Pause*)
Which isn't about you. I just need to be lost for awhile.

(CHARLIE *absorbs.*)

SUE: (*Simple*) I like order, Charlie. But for the last six weeks I've sat next to you, and I've gone with it. Chalked it up to faith. Told myself that the impropriety of what you're doing was maybe ultimately worth it.
(*Pause*)
Which is maybe also true of this. Leaving James, answering your call last night...are reminders of who I can be. Of a power I forgot I had. Even if I lose my way as I find it.
(*Pause*)
So I don't need anything from you. Other than the very nice reminder of last night. I don't even need coffee.

(SUE *smiles, a little goofily, as* CHARLIE *takes this all in.*)

CHARLIE: Fair enough.

SUE: I can't imagine you're upset.

CHARLIE: *(He is)* Ah…No. I'm okay.

SUE: *(Beat)* Are you gonna leave Channel 10?

CHARLIE: I don't know.
(Pause)
They offered me four million dollars. And that's just to join the network and move to New York.

SUE: But you think it's real?

CHARLIE: *Some* part of it is. "The world is moving" and they want me on board. I think they wanna work with me, develop the platform, and then, yeah—put me in.
(Pause)
And they're not wrong to think big. I mean the world's a fucking shit-show. We're killing each other: Robbing the poor, gutting the earth, bombing weddings, sawing off heads, drinking *coffee* as little kids get raped. We're not *living* right. Even if *we're* not doing all that, even if we're just witnesses, it's still criminal. And so if some guy at the head of a fifty billion dollar media conglomerate has the balls to *try* to make a dent in all that, then shouldn't I at least be open to it?

SUE: …Maybe.
(Pause)
But I'm curious: Do you think you're actually…*touched.*

CHARLIE: *(Pause; a small smile…)* I guess it's…possible; that I'm some sort of…vehicle.

(SUE nods slowly; then kisses CHARLIE on the cheek.)

SUE: Good luck, Charles.

(Lights shift. CHARLIE now alone on stage with CASEY, who is in a wheelchair. Beat. Then—)

CHARLIE: Quite a couple days.

CASEY: Yeah.

CHARLIE: How're you feeling?

CASEY: Tell the truth I don't remember much between today and when I got beat.

CHARLIE: But you've watched the news?

CASEY: *(A nod)* Plus all the nurses told me. They think you're some sorta God.

CHARLIE: Well. Two days ago they wouldn't even let me visit.

CASEY: Funny like that.

CHARLIE: ...So, what do *you* think about it all?

CASEY: You asking if I think you're God?

CHARLIE: No. I'm just curious what your reaction is, to suddenly getting better like that.

CASEY: I don't have a reaction, I was unconscious.

CHARLIE: But from what you've heard.

CASEY: Different ways to interpret I guess. One doctor I talked to was like, "People come outta comas all the time. It ain't a miracle, it's just a good doctor and some luck."

(CHARLIE *considers this.*)

CHARLIE: Could be that too.

CASEY: I'm just saying, he's gotta point: People *do* wake up.

CHARLIE: Right.

CASEY: ...You takin' that job?

CHARLIE: What—the, ah—?

CASEY: Your own show or whatever.

CHARLIE: Thinking about it.

CASEY: *Take* that shit.

CHARLIE: Why?

CASEY: Get the fuck outta Rochester.

CHARLIE: You think?

CASEY: You get to say what you want, get paid like a motherfucker, take on mad respect. It's religion, man: Push forward, don't look back, *fulfillment*.

(Pause)

CHARLIE: And what about you? You gonna push on? Now that you have a second chance?

CASEY: ...Nope.

CHARLIE: Why not?

CASEY: 'Cause in three days I'm goin' right back in that cell. Nothin' to push on *to*. I mean, you leave it up to me, I just as soon you'd lemme die. I ain't need to be livin' like a dog for the next fifty years. An' I ain't tryin' to disrespect you, but all you did was put me back behind bars. An' there ain't no God in a jail cell.

CHARLIE: ...But don't people find God in jail cells all the time?

CASEY: That ain't God, man, it's just niggas' lookin' for somethin' to do.
(He turns and starts to wheel himself away.)
Nurse said I only had five minutes.

CHARLIE: Casey, I was just wondering if there was anything you'd like me to pass on—

CASEY: Naw, man, I ain't gonna give you that.

CHARLIE: Give me what?

CASEY: Whatever you're lookin' for—a fuckin' victory lap.

CHARLIE: That's not what I—

CASEY: An' I ain't gonna turn all holy just 'cause some rich white dude prayed for me on T V. I ain't no one-

time fuckin' guilt relief for you, man. I gotta live here
probably 'til I *die*, so I ain't gonna *"find the Good Lord"*
just so you can point at me an' say, "See, there's one
*other muh*fucker that I saved." *I ain't fuckin' saved.* I'm
dead, man. *This ain't no game!*—

CHARLIE: Look, I'm sorry you feel—

CASEY: What'd you even *come* here for? A handshake?
Is that why your friend ain't here? 'Cause you want all
the credit yourself?

CHARLIE: I'm just trying to help—

CASEY: Naw, man—*I ain't no fuckin' trophy nigger!*
(And then, over his shoulder as he leaves)
I'll see you on the tube.

(CHARLIE stands—)

(Lights shift—)

*(Projections shows RON in glorious stand-up reportorial
splendor—)*

RON: As you might guess, the communal *exuberance*
following Charles Duff's *physiological redemption* of
Casey Simmons—and I don't mean to embarrass
Charles but that's what some are calling it here on
the lively streets of Rochester—that exuberance is
palpable, and yet *tempered* by rumors of his departure
for pastures more green and global than our own.

*(Cut to a blue-collar ROCHESTER RESIDENT in an on-the-
street interview:)*

ROCHESTER RESIDENT: If the guy wants to cash out I
can't blame him, so long as he's cashing out in a way
that keeps us honest.

(An OLDER WOMAN:)

OLDER WOMAN: *Rochester needs you, Charlie! Do not turn
away from thy own flesh and blood!*

(*Cut to a* CHINESE MAN—)

CHINESE MAN: It doesn't matter where he goes. God is
everywhere. God is Buzzfeed, God is Snapchat, God is
TikTok in my head.

(*Back to* RON *in his stand-up.*)

RON: Well, not sure what to say about that. But what I
did do is gather my own religious *"focus group"*, and I
asked these scholars what *they* thought Charles should
do:

(*Three religious scholars seated on folding chairs in a high
school gymnasium.*)

OLD TALMUDIC SCHOLAR: In the *Mishnah* we say
l'takken olam b'malkhut Shaddai: "To heal the world
under God's sovereignty." *Heal, repair, perfect?* —No
matter how you dice it— *Just keep going Charlie!*

(*Cut to* RON, *nodding. Then:*)

PRIEST: *I needed clothes and you clothed me; I was sick and
you looked after me; I was in prison and you came to visit.*
(*Straight into the camera*)
Duff is doing God's work. It is simple, it is intimate,
and it is paradoxical to think it can be done on a larger
scale.

(*Cut to* RON, *nodding. Then:*)

KORANIC SCHOLAR: The Koran tells us to *exhort people to
kindness.* This is what he is doing. Exhorting people to
kindness.
(*Into camera*)
Exhort as many as you can.

(*Cut to* RON, *holding back tears. Then—back to him in
stand-up.*)

RON: So as you can see: *Rochester stands divided!*
(*And then*)

Now—I did *not* talk to a Buddhist, and I'm sorry.
(Perhaps a small bow of the head; then—)
From the streets of Rochester, this is Ron Kirkpatrick.

(The projection ends, lights shift.)

(CHARLIE and JOHN are alone on stage, perhaps at a park, perhaps on a bench, each holding a can of beer.)

CHARLIE: So…you gonna tell me where you been?

JOHN: I just needed some time.

CHARLIE: I was worried. Thought you might be hanging out with the Razorsharks.

JOHN: Sorry.

CHARLIE: But you're doing better?

JOHN: Much.

CHARLIE: Yeah?

JOHN: Yeah. I mean, you treat this shit, you talk about it, try to turn it into some sorta…*knowledge.* It never goes away, but—it sometimes gets better.

CHARLIE: Good.
(Pause)
You, ah…been following the news?

JOHN: *(A smile)* Yeah. You're fucking awesome, man.

CHARLIE: No I'm not—

JOHN: You are. I mean I have no idea how you *did* that, or *if* you did it, but whatever happened, keep making it happen.

CHARLIE: I'll try—

JOHN: Sky's the fucking limit, Charlie.

CHARLIE: Well, it's not like I got Casey out of prison.

(JOHN nods…)

CHARLIE: I saw him yesterday. He basically told me I was useless.

JOHN: You're not. But I can see why he'd say that. He's still one of the forgotten ones.

CHARLIE: …You coming back to work?

JOHN: Be there tonight.

CHARLIE: You had enough time?

JOHN: Yeah. You know…sometimes sad people just… go away; to an unreachable place. And just hide there. You know?

(Pause)

But if they're lucky, sometimes they manage to send like a, a dispatch, back to the normal world; with the hope that someone's standing there with his hand out, looking for letters from really fucked up people.

(Pause)

And so what keeps a lotta people like *me* in the game… are people like *you*. Who they're able to contact. So it's actually *you* people, who end up saving some of *us*; instead of just passing us by.

(Pause)

So just keep doing that, Charlie. Keep standing there with your hand out, looking for the letter. 'Cause it's appreciated.

(Beat; and then)

…Just the theory of a melancholic sportscaster.

(CHARLIE takes this in, appreciative. He stands.)

CHARLIE: Thanks, man.

JOHN: Thank *you*.

(CHARLIE and JOHN shake…)

CHARLIE: See you in a bit?

JOHN: Absolutely.

(Lights shift—)

(—and we are in the news room. SUE *enters.)*

SUE: Hi.

CHARLIE: Hi.

SUE: We okay?

CHARLIE: You mean do I mind that you used my body for your own private religious self-empowerment? No problem.

SUE: That's not what it was.

CHARLIE: ...It would've been nice; to explore.

SUE: You could have any woman out there with a shred of spiritual belief.

CHARLIE: And yet I would've chosen you.

SUE: ...Lying is a sacrilege.

CHARLIE: It's not a lie.

(Beat)

Have you and James told your son you're leaving?

SUE: *(A nod)* He's freaking out, but... So is James for that matter.

CHARLIE: But it's for the better?

SUE: Yes.

(Pause)

Did you decide about the job?

*(*CHARLIE *nods)*

SUE: ...Congratulations.

CHARLIE: *(Pause)* You disapprove.

SUE: Not for me to say.

CHARLIE: But why? What is it that—?

SUE: Because people can't play God, Charlie. *It will eventually corrupt.* Which is not to say I know the

answers, or that the religions of the world—very much
including my own—aren't occasionally savage to the
core. But I do believe that the work to be done is quiet;
it is careful; and it is here. Blind as we may be.

CHARLIE: ...Point taken.

(ZOELLNER *enters, looking like a ghost.* CHARLIE *and* SUE
take note. Beat)

ZOELLNER: I think we have a problem with John.

(*Lights shift...sound...*)

(*Light finds* CHARLIE *alone, as he sinks to his knees...
Silence*)

(*After several moments, he reaches for his phone. Looks at it
and sees he has a message. He listens:*)

(*—as we hear the message:*)

LISA: (*O S*) Charlie, it's Lisa. You missed Rick's concert
Thursday night. I just thought you should know.
(*Pause*)
You're fucking unbelievable.

(*LISA hangs up.* CHARLIE's *eyes close....*)

(*—then he lifts himself up from the floor.*)

(*Lights shift and he is now with* RICK, *outside* RICK's
house.)

CHARLIE: I'm so sorry.
(*And then*)
I got...there was a lot happening...and I messed up.
(*And then*)
I have no excuse.
(*Pause*)
I know I've been a shitty Dad. And that you probably
think I haven't changed. Which maybe I haven't. But
I will find a way to be there for you. I swear to you I
will.

(Pause)

Rick? Please.

(No answer)

CHARLIE: Please don't cut me out.

(Pause)

I love you. You have to know how much I love you.

RICK: It doesn't matter.

CHARLIE: Yes it does—

RICK: It doesn't.

(Pause, as CHARLIE *turns slightly away, bending over, hands on knees, unable to speak.)*

RICK: What's the matter with you?

CHARLIE: There's a…John Ebbs is missing. He was seen walking along the cliffs this morning. And then the person who saw him lost sight of him.

*(*RICK *finally looks at* CHARLIE.*)*

CHARLIE: They called the station because they'd recognized him.

*(*RICK *is paying full attention…)*

CHARLIE: We haven't been able to reach him.

RICK: What do you think happened?

CHARLIE: I don't know.

*(*RICK *waits for more.)*

RICK: Why would he…?

CHARLIE: Depression is a disease. Which cripples people—

RICK: But *why?*

CHARLIE: I don't know.

RICK: *(Beat…)* Is it the same cliff where you and me walked that time?

CHARLIE: …Yes.

RICK: *People aren't supposed to jump off cliffs, Dad!*

CHARLIE: …No; they're not.

(Beat)

RICK: So why are you fucking standing here?

(No answer)

RICK: You need to pray that they find him.

CHARLIE: I dunno, Rick. This one may be…

RICK: But isn't that what this whole thing's about?

(CHARLIE looks at RICK.)

CHARLIE: I don't actually know.

RICK: But it's what you do.

CHARLIE: Yes—

RICK: So shouldn't you do a miracle for him? I mean… *isn't that who you became?*

CHARLIE: …As opposed to what?

(RICK doesn't answer. CHARLIE steps toward him, to comfort—)

CHARLIE: Rick—

RICK: Get away.

(He has stepped back, suppressing sadness, rage, not sure which.)

He's the only friend you have and you can't even do *that?*

CHARLIE: We're trying to find him—

RICK: No you're not, you're *here!*

CHARLIE: Rick—

RICK: Pray for him to come back!

(Trying not to cry)

It's what you're good at.

(CHARLIE tries to hold RICK—)

CHARLIE: Rick, come here—

RICK: *Get OFF me!! —You don't get to do that!*

(RICK has shoved CHARLIE away. CHARLIE stands, frozen—)

RICK: *Do something!*

CHARLIE: Rick—

RICK: *Help him!*

CHARLIE: I can't, Rick—I can't do that—

RICK: *Why not?*

CHARLIE: I don't know.

RICK: *(Breaking) MAKE HIM FUCKING COME BACK!—*

CHARLIE: Rick—

(CHARLIE has reached RICK and struggles to hold him as RICK shoves him away—but CHARLIE holds tight, almost overpowering, containing him in a hug—)

CHARLIE: It's okay, Rick—

RICK: No it's not—

CHARLIE: You're right, it's not. It's not okay.

(Fighting to hold RICK)

CHARLIE: It's not okay. It's not okay.

(RICK continues struggling but CHARLIE doesn't let go. Slowly CHARLIE wins, and RICK lets himself be held, perhaps crying silently…)

CHARLIE: It's not okay. …It's not okay.

(…Silence)

(RICK *continues to let himself be held... But then he steps away...*)

(CHARLIE *and* RICK *regard each other. Then—*)

RICK: It's probably too late.
(*He turns and leaves.*)

(CHARLIE *stands alone. After a moment, he lowers his head, closes his eyes, and perhaps tries a silent prayer...or maybe he's crying. Hard to say*)

(*Finally he looks up. Beat. He starts to walk—*)

(*—as lights shift...and a version of the show's opening music begins, as* CHARLIE *steps behind the desk.* SUE, *and* ZOELLNER *stand to the side, watching.*)

(*Lights shift and he is now on air:*)

CHARLIE: (*Very simple*) Good evening.
(*Pause*)
Our colleague John Ebbs took his own life this afternoon. His body was found an hour ago along the banks of the Genesee River, here in his beloved Rochester.
(*Pause*)
I, ah…..
(*Pause*)
Just before we came on the air, my co-anchor Sue Raspell recited a verse to me from the Bible that… seemed to make sense, at least for a moment, to us both: *Two are better than one; because they have a good reward for their toil. For if they fall, one will lift up his fellow. But woe to him who is alone when he falls and has not another to lift him up.*
(*Pause*)
Sue said this in regard to my son, who was in need of an answer earlier today. And for whom all I wanted was to be there. So he would not be alone.
(*Pause*)

John Ebbs *was* alone; and he *did* fall, with no one there
to catch him. And prayer, or faith, has no answer to
that. At least not right now; not for me. All we can do,
all *I* can do…is be there for those still here. For my
son, who I love and who I hope will allow me to father
him as we stumble through life. And for the others
I've been lucky enough to encounter over these last six
weeks.

(Pause)

Which is why I won't be leaving Channel 10. For me,
for now, this is sufficient reward for my toil. Blind
though I may be.

(Pause)

Good night.

(Lights shift, as—)

*(—as the news desk disappears and for the first time the
stage is completely empty but for a shaft of light; and
CHARLIE.)*

(Silence)

(Sound of a prison cell slamming shut.)

*(A moment later, CASEY enters, still in his prison jumpsuit,
holding a bag of Fritos. He comes to a stop…and takes
CHARLIE in.)*

CASEY: Didn't think I'd see you again.

CHARLIE: Yeah, well…

(CASEY and CHARLIE sit. Silence…)

CHARLIE: They told me you got a work detail.

CASEY: Yeah, in the print shop but today's my day off.

CHARLIE: Wednesday's your day of rest?

CASEY: I guess.

CHARLIE: So it's a good day for me to come by? In
general?

(CASEY *takes this in.*)

CASEY: I guess.

(Beat)

Is it a long drive?

CHARLIE: Not too bad.

(CASEY and CHARLIE sit... Beat...)

CASEY: You wanna Frito?

CHARLIE: Sure.

(CHARLIE takes a Frito. CASEY and CHARLIE chew.)

(As lights fade to black...)

END OF PLAY